Invest to Prosper

Invest to Prosper

Clint W Sorenson, CFA®, CMT®
Robert A Leggett, CFA®, CFP®, JD

ISBN: 0692443525
ISBN 13: 9780692443521
Library of Congress Control Number: 2015907246
Emerald IP, Cary, NC

Table of Contents

About the Authors

Clint Sorenson, CFA®, CMT® is a managing partner and portfolio manager for Emerald Investment Partners, LLC and the co-founder of WealthShield. He has developed and currently manages proprietary quantitative strategies by fusing together behavioral finance, fundamental and technical analysis.

He is a Chartered Market Technician and Chartered Financial Analyst and is proficient in a broad range of investment topics. He has written extensively on the markets and is a contributor on several well-known financial websites.

Clint earned his bachelor's degree from the University of North Carolina-Chapel Hill. He is also a board member and current Vice President of the CFA Society North Carolina.

Robert Leggett, CFA®, CFP®, JD has more than thirty years of experience in the financial services industry and business world. He is a managing partner and portfolio manager for Emerald Investment Partners, LLC and the co-founder of WealthShield.

Robert has extensive experience in legal, tax, real estate and accounting disciplines and served as the CEO of a $300 million family business.

He earned his bachelor's degree from Emory University and his Juris Doctor from the T.C. Williams School of Law at the University of Richmond. He is a Chartered Financial Analyst and a Certified Financial Planner™ practitioner.

Acknowledgments

We would like to express our deepest gratitude to our families for continuing to support our work so enthusiastically. This book would have never been completed without your trust, confidence, and commitment.

Julia Sefler, Caroline Leggett, David Stefanick, Luke Vernon, Edward Threlfall, Harrison Gillette, and Grier Rubeling spent countless hours researching, editing, deliberating, testing, and compiling. Your work is much appreciated and deserves mention.

Finally, we would like to thank our clients and friends who rely on our expertise in extremely uncertain times. You are the inspiration for the ideas in this book.

Preface

The vast majority of investors that come to us seeking our advice have been devastated financially and emotionally by the two 50 percent declines in the stock market in the past fifteen years. They want to grow their wealth without experiencing another severe stock market meltdown. If you share similar fears but need your investment portfolio to grow over time, this book is for you.

After scouring pages and pages of academic research and experimenting with various disciplines during our careers, we crafted a process that we are assured will work to protect investors from massive market declines while at the same time allowing liberal participation in the upside of asset markets. By providing protection during declines and offering growth during rising markets, our disciplined approach allows investors to stick to their plan while generating better odds of success.

In this book, we take you on a brief journey through some interesting historical periods where markets both rose and fell in spectacular fashion. Although financial media will have you believe that periods of market stress are unforeseeable, we illustrate the contrary. We show you how to apply the same principles that have helped make many of the most notable investors so successful over their careers. This book helps prepare you to win in the stock market by having a method to protect against the vicious downside.

Bear Bryant, the famous coach, once stated that "offense fills the seats, but defense wins championships." We believe this saying applies equally to investing. It is no wonder that Warren Buffett's rules of investing are as follows:

Rule number one: "Don't lose money."
Rule number two: "Don't forget the first rule."

We don't believe that Warren Buffett believes it is possible to invest without losing money. He has had plenty of losses in his career. We do believe that he makes an incredible point about risk. Controlling your losses is an important aspect of proper portfolio management. This book provides you with a time-tested discipline for cutting losses short and taking calculated risks. Most investors become overly fixated on the growth potential of the market without adequately preparing for the inevitable market declines. By the end of this book, you will be confident in your ability to protect and grow your wealth in both good markets and bad.

The Federal Reserve and other global central banks have propped up asset prices over the last decade. They have introduced massive amounts of monetary stimulus, created negative real interest rates, and changed accounting practices in order to prevent the market and financial system from imploding. Their actions have been largely responsible for the current bubble in the stock market.

Human psychology guarantees that bubbles will form and bubbles will pop. As market prices rise precipitously, the crowds become euphoric, pushing prices up further. This type of behavior creates a positive feedback mechanism that produces price distortions. Prices move higher than are justified by the underlying fundamentals fashioning an asset bubble.

You do not have to dig too deep into the memory bank to recollect past bubbles. The technology bubble of the late 1990s, the real estate bubble of 2003–2007, and now the central-bank bubble have all taken asset prices to new highs. The problem is that these bubbles end in gruesome fashion.

The technology bubble ended with a 50 percent crash in the S&P 500 and a 75 percent crash in the NASDAQ. The real estate bubble ended with a 50 percent crash in the S&P 500 and a complete credit freeze. We are now six years into another massive bubble, facilitated by record amounts of stimulus, bailouts, and zero percent interest rates. The time to arm yourself with the tools to protect your wealth against the coming crash is now.

Introduction

When we set out to write this book, our mission was simple. We wanted to provide an easy-to-follow guide to managing your investments in both up and down markets. As experts in the investment industry, we have constructed portfolios for private clients, institutions, and other financial professionals. In our experience, we found that investors want all of the upside and none of the down. In any business—investment management being no different—giving the customer what he or she wants is the name of the game. Therefore, our task is to generate programs that grow wealth similar to aggressive strategies with a conservative amount of risk.

Financial theory suggests that there must be a trade-off between risk and reward. In other words, if you want huge returns, you have to take huge risks. In this book, we hope to demonstrate that this is not the case. You can generate market-beating returns with significantly less risk than the market. Furthermore, you can do this while investing in index funds that track the market. It sounds too good to be true, but we assure you that it is not only possible but simple to apply and manage.

No one can control the market movements— no matter how smart we are, we do not get to decide if the markets go up or down. Financial media pundits would have you believe that the so-called experts have some sort of handle on the day-to-day market action, but in reality, the experts are often guessing. As human beings, we fear the unexpected. We have an aversion to ambiguity that leads us to tune in to CNBC or Bloomberg regularly, searching for answers. The variables that appear to alter the markets each day are too numerous to fathom, leading many investors to turn their money over to the professionals or experts.

Financial media want you to believe that investing is complex, difficult, and only for the brilliant. The primary outlets for financial information are driven largely by ratings, so they attempt to create a dependency on their programs, enticing you to believe that your success is correlated to how much information you devour. Our process will allow you to take back control of your investments and your life. You will no longer have to remain glued to the TV or computer screen, searching for the next best stock tip. Instead, you will be able to invest in the markets knowing that you have a technique that is dynamic and adaptive.

Two important factors to worry about when investing are the risk you take and the fees you pay. These factors are critical to your success. The amount of risk you take is all about your asset mix, or how much you invest among stocks, bonds, and cash. The problem is that investors and academics misunderstand risk. Understanding your unique tolerance for risk is critical to staying the course when investing. The reason centers on how investors are emotionally wired to think about money. If you take too much risk, and your asset mix is not on par with your ability and willingness to tolerate risk, you will often make poor decisions. On the contrary, if you do not take enough risk, you will most likely not reach your desired outcomes.

Your investment costs are often the most overlooked factor and can have a damaging effect on outcomes. Our procedure cuts through all the marketing gimmicks and compensation schemes and instead focuses on traditional asset classes (stocks and bonds) with the use of index funds. Index funds are low cost, transparent, and tax efficient, giving investors the opportunity to participate in the markets in an efficient manner.

Let's think for a minute about what might be the most important factor to control when investing. If you thought about behavior, you are right. When most investors invest, they are solely focused on the markets themselves, getting wrapped up in the day-to-day fluctuations. The stock market tends to lead the investor (and professional) through a whipsaw of emotions. One day the market is up, and the investor is on top of the world; the next day it is down, and the investor needs an antidepressant. Benjamin Graham, the father of value investing, stated it best when he said, "Individuals who cannot master their emotions are ill suited to profit from the investment process."[1]

Our tactics are designed to help you build a behaviorally congruent portfolio. The focus is on implementing a quantitative asset allocation discipline that allows investors to control their asset mix in a fashion that takes advantage of mass market psychology and shields the portfolio against the common cognitive biases we all possess. The purpose is to give you a course for controlling your behavior in both the up and down markets, giving you a better chance of success. Our method is broken down into two systems that combine to form an overall strategy.

The first system is a value-based system called the Value Allocator. The essence of this system is to invest in assets when they are cheap and

---

1 Benjamin Graham, *The Intelligent Investor* (New York: Harper Collins, 1973).

sell them when they are expensive. This is what we call a buy-low, sell-high system. The second system is our tactical program that is based on momentum or trend following. This system is our buy-high, sell-higher system. We know these systems seem counterintuitive at the moment, but we will demonstrate how they combine beautifully in the context of a lively market. We will analyze major historical market movements from the early nineteen hundreds to give you a feel for different market environments and how the approach adjusts and adapts. We will also provide various enhancements that can be applied to generate an optimal portfolio design.

The book is conveniently structured to begin with the empirical explanation for why our style has worked and then end with why it will continue to be effective in the future. Investors can achieve impressive results by intelligently controlling costs, risks, and behavior. We will cut through years of exhausting research to provide you with a strategy that is designed to protect your portfolio against large market declines and grow your wealth.

Control Your Behavior

Investing according to our gut is a bad strategy when attempting to master the markets. Behaviorally, we are wired to make poor decisions when it comes to money. In fact, neuroscientists have uncovered evidence that suggests that money is like a drug. Receiving money has nearly an identical neurological response as if one were to subject themselves to a dose of cocaine. Human beings look at money as a reward and the antici- pation of that reward results in a release of dopa- mine. Dopamine is the same neurotransmitter responsible for taking a cocaine user to a high.[2] As human beings, we should not trust our intuition for making decisions as the "high" experienced can challenge sound judgement.

Financial experts are even more prone to mak- ing erroneous decisions because of their overcon- fidence and the illusion of skill. Peter Lynch, in his book *One Up on Wall Street*, told investors to use their life experiences to help them pick stocks. His message broadly appealed to the investing pub- lic, as his approach exuded simplicity and com- mon sense. Peter Lynch had the wind at his back when he published this book, having been in a stock market that moved up in relentless fashion since valuations bottomed in 1982. Although the advice sounded good, buying what you know is hardly viable for all market environments.

When markets are overpriced, it seldom makes sense to buy anything, as the overall market has a tendency to pull the best stocks down with it.

---

2 James Montier, *Behavioural Investing: A Practitioner's Guide to Applying Behavioural Finance* (West Sussex, England: John Wiley & Sons Ltd., 2007).

During Peter Lynch's day, the philosophy of a rising tide lifts all boats characterized the majority of investors' attitudes toward markets. There are several other strategies that are equally as useless as Lynch's recommended approach. The most useless of the bunch is trying to time the market based on the news of the day or a Wall Street rumor. Let's face it: by the time you have the news, the price probably reflects the information. You might as well assume that you are the last market participant to receive any such news or rumors.

Financial media have manifested the idea that people actually know what is going on in the market. On any given day, there are several different opinions as to why the market went up, down, or sideways. The fact is that all of the opinions are just that—opinions. Gray Davis, a trader profiled in Michael Covel's book *The Little Book of Trading: Trend Following Strategy for Big Winnings*, stated it best: "You don't make money by explaining how things happen and you don't make money by guessing what's going to happen in the future. You don't know what's going to happen in the future. The things that occur in the future that make you money are all things you couldn't figure out were going to happen."

Market prognosticators do not know what is going to happen or even why something has happened. All they can do is tell you what has happened. Human beings are inherently horrible at forecasting, yet investors continue to cling to every guru or market seer that arises. For example, Jim Cramer, the host of *Mad Money* on CNBC, has risen to stardom over the past decade by promising investors the discovery of a "bull market somewhere." Investors hang on every word, listening eagerly to the man they assume to be a stock market expert. The show is quite entertaining, as he uses interesting props and noises, and he appears to be quite knowledgeable. The problem is that the show itself facilitates short-term focus and herd behavior. There is even a name for the short-term effect on a stock caused by Cramer's recommendations: the Cramer Effect. This effect causes stocks to gain popularity after a stock is mentioned favorably on Cramer's show, *Mad Money.*

Interestingly, Cramer does not have the best track record of demonstrating forecasting ability. One does not need to go further than evaluating the speech he gave in February of 2000. The title was "The Winners of the New World" and featured Cramer's top-ten stock picks. His choices were as follows: 724 Solutions, Ariba, Digital Island, Exodus, Infospace.com, Inktomi, Mercury Interactive, Sonera, Verisign, and Veritas Software. Investors who followed these recommendations would have been virtually wiped out. Only one of the companies is still in existence today—Verisign—but it is more than 70 percent below its peak value.

Experts are no better than anyone else at making predictions. As Michael Covel, best-selling author and trend following crusader states, "We really can't predict. Econometric researchers have tried to forecast or predict where markets were supposedly headed for decades, but they continually fail." Therefore, making decisions based on what you or some expert thinks is going to happen is not the way to success.

Investors need a discipline to follow day in and day out. Our recommendation is to determine simple rules to follow and stay diligent in following them. Investing is not about being right. Instead, it is "about winning in the long run."[3] It sounds easy, but it is extremely difficult to follow a boring practice through the short-term randomness of the market. There are times when any system faces challenges. A string of bad outcomes could easily have the strongest of investors doubting the merits of a thorough program. This is called playing your results. Investors believe that if they make money, they are using a good idea, and if they lose money, they are using a bad idea. You cannot play the results; instead you have to try to make an assessment of the

---

3 Michael Covel, *The Little Book of Trading: Trend Following Strategy for Big Winnings* (Hoboken, NJ: John Wiley & Sons Inc., 2011).

odds and make the most appropriate decision given those odds.

You have to know what you are going to do ahead of time. You must understand your process and adhere to your discipline when the market goes up, down, or sideways. We recommend having these decisions made before putting a dollar at risk. What are you going to trade? What is your signal to buy? When do you get out if you have made a profit? When would you exit a position if the market moves against you? How much money do you risk? Knowing the answers to these questions allows you to approach the markets in a prepared fashion. This book exists to provide a mechanism for investing in uncertain markets through a simple, rules-based approach to asset allocation.

Asset Allocation Is What Matters

Deciding how much to invest in stocks bonds, cash and other asset classes is imperative. In two different studies, one by Brinson, Hood, and Gilbert in 1986 and the other by Ibbotson and Kaplan in 2000, the researchers concluded that asset allocation decisions are responsible for a majority of the returns generated by managers. If the asset mix is responsible for a majority of the returns, this decision should become the focus.

Positioning the portfolio to be in the "right place at the right time" is far more important than finding the right stock to buy.[4] According to financial theory, investors should position assets that will not move together in a portfolio to minimize the portfolio's volatility. Instead, our view is that one should apply simple, quantitative rules that determine how much and when to allocate to various asset classes.

"The Hedgehog and the Fox" is a famous essay by Isaiah Berlin in which he divides the world into hedgehogs and foxes. The fox is a complex creature—cunning and knowledgeable about different strategies when it comes to attacking the hedgehog. At first glance, the fox looks like the eventual winner of the predator-prey situation. However, the hedgehog is rather simple, looking to gather food and protecting his home. When the fox attacks, the hedgehog can roll up into a ball with sharp spikes all over his body to fend off the attack. No matter how many times the attacks take place, the hedgehog knows how to defend with incredible effectiveness. The fox, on the other hand, is always calculating, recalculating, calibrating, and recalibrating, attempting to determine the perfect attack plan.

---

4 Bill Bonner and Will Bonner, *Family Fortunes: How to Build Family Wealth and Hold on to It for 100 Years* (New York: John Wiley & Sons, 2012).

Berlin characterized people as either foxes or hedgehogs based on the fact that foxes "see the world in all its complexity" while hedgehogs simplify a complex world into a basic principle that guides everything.[5] Wall Street is equipped with enough foxes. High-frequency trading, algorithmic programs, credit default swaps, complex derivatives, arbitrage trading, and the like are all extremely complex and baffling to the majority of market participants. You have to be a hedgehog to succeed in the market. You must be able to derive a simple unifying concept that will drive your decision-making—a concept that will allow you to build a rules-based program that you can follow with discipline.

With the amount of money poured into research, technology, and academics, it is going to be hard to be the best at security selection. On the other hand, the governing financial theory of most allocation methods is rather antiquated. Therefore, there must exist an "edge" to be realized. Realizing your limitations and facing the facts about your abilities is an important step in being intellectually honest. Wall Street has a leg up on the average investor when it comes to many of the areas where edges can be derived; luckily, asset allocation is not one of them.

---

5 Jim Collins, *Good to Great: Why Some Companies Make the Leap and Others Don't* (New York: HarperCollins, 2001).

Determine Your Unique Asset Mix

Deciding the proper asset mix is the "least costly and the most valuable" decision.[6] Financial objectives, risk tolerance, tax and legal considerations, liquidity need, time horizon, and any other constraints help guide the decision. You need to ask yourself the following questions:

- How much money do I need to have to reach my goals?
- How much pain can I tolerate to get there?
- How long do I have to invest?
- How reliant am I on my investments currently?
- What could potentially hold me back?

Most of these questions are easy to define with introspection. Risk tolerance is not so self-explanatory, yet it is critically important. As investors, we hate losses. They are a painful irritant that can often skew our judgment and scare us into altering our plan. Risk tolerance should be split into two separate but mutually dependent components—ability and willingness. Ability refers to how much risk you *can* take. Willingness refers to how much risk you *want to* take. The prudent

---

6 Charles D. Ellis, *Winning the Loser's Game: Timeless Strategies for Successful Investing* (New York: McGraw Hill, 2010).

investor would weigh both components and take the most conservative.

Imagine for a second that you had a willingness to take a moderate amount of risk. However, upon inspection of your current situation you determined that you only had an ability to take a conservative amount of risk. Your stated risk tolerance would be conservative. Risk tolerance helps you determine the plausibility of your objectives within the context of your other stated constraints.

We recommend documenting your objectives, constraints, and risk tolerance in a formal investment policy statement (IPS). The IPS is a wonderful tool for accountability and should provide for flexibility in the investment mix to account for varying market dynamics. The IPS will also include the portfolio construction guidelines. It is important to revisit your IPS during periods of extreme market movements to help you focus on your long-term goals and stick to your plan. The IPS should be an adaptable document that changes as your situation evolves.

The CFA Institute, a nonprofit member organization for Chartered Financial Analysts, has a great guide on their website for creating an investment policy statement. For more information, please visit www.cfainstitute.org and view the section "For Investors" under the "Insights and Learning" tab.

An intelligent investor's approach begins with a thorough understanding of self. Ask yourself what you want out of the market and how much pain you can take and have a clear understanding of what your financial picture looks like. Once you understand where you want to go and what may hold you back, figuring out the *how* is relatively simple.

CHAPTER 1

Value Investing- The Core

> Above all, avoid
> big mistakes.
> — WARREN BUFFETT

Avoiding Big Mistakes

There is an old Wall Street axiom claiming that the stock market takes the stairs up and the window down. After an impressive rally of over 132 percent since the 2009 bottom, correction calls are emerging. Market participants are nervous—for good reason. US stock valuations are in the top 3 percent of the historical observations, which usually indicates low returns will be forthcoming over the next ten years. The Federal Reserve is winding down the massive stimulus program and is targeting rate increases as of the writing of this book. Furthermore, the US economy continues to muddle along at subpar growth (below 2 percent) and has yet to garner the escape velocity necessary to remove the training wheels. Despite the head-winds, demand has been strong for US equities.

In the United States, the Dow Jones Industrial Average has had ten historic declines of greater than 40 percent. There have been thirty declines in excess of 20 percent. Risk happens faster and more frequently than finance theory suggests. Statistically speaking, the market returns have historically been fat tailed, meaning there is a larger frequency of extreme events than would be predicted by a normal distribution. In order to achieve better-than-average market returns, it is critical that investors employ a method that mitigates the risk of suffering the all-too-frequent large declines.

Investors are nervous that another crash could wipe out the gains that took five years to muster. Time is supposed to heal, but 2008 did a number on the average investor—so any threat to revisit the painful memories of that time may cause investors to act in an erratic fashion. The fear of losses allows for the negative feedback loops of the market to materialize with greater speed than bull markets.

There are several different definitions of what constitutes a bull or bear market. One popular definition of a bear market is one in which prices have fallen 20 percent from the previous high. The fact that a stock or a market has fallen 20 percent has no meaning without a contextual backdrop. A stock could decline 20 percent and still be in an uptrend or bull market. A bull or bear market should be defined within the context of the overall trend.

There are two types of bull and bear markets, cyclical and secular. Cyclical markets are shorter term in nature. The average cyclical bull market tends to last close to four years, while a bear market lasts two years. Cyclical markets are not the focus of our work. This book is more about identifying the long-term opportunities and avoiding large blunders.

Year	Market Milestone	Percent Change	Number of Years	Annualized Return, No Dividends	Annualized Return with Dividends
1877	Low	-	-	-	-
1906	High	383%	29.3	5.1%	10.1%
1921	Low	-69%	14.9	-7.5%	-2.0%
1929	High	396%	8.1	21.9%	28.4%
1932	Low	-81%	2.7	-44.9%	-41.2%
1937	High	266%	4.7	32.1%	38.7%
1949	Low	-54%	12.3	-6.2%	-0.8%
1968	High	413%	19.5	8.8%	13.3%
1982	Low	-63%	13.6	-7.0%	-3.0%
2000	High	666%	18.1	11.9%	15.3%
2009	Low	-59%	8.5	-9.8%	-8.1%
Now	-	128%	5.6	N/A	N/A

Based on inflation-adjusted S&P Composite monthly averages of daily closes.

Figure 1: Bull and Bear markets.
Source: Doug Short

Capturing the secular (long-term) trends in stocks should be the focus for investors. To be less vague, investors should avoid the secular declines and capture the secular up trends. As students of bear markets, we have found that most historical bear markets decline in stages, allowing for a well-designed program to become defensive.

Each secular bull market lasts, on average, almost sixteen years, while the secular bear markets average roughly ten. The up markets gain an average of 415 percent, while the down periods decline by an average of 65 percent (see Figure 1). Every investor should aim to build a portfolio that can weather the secular market declines and capture the market advances.

Daniel Kahneman and Amos Taversky stated that a loss is felt about two-and-a-half times more than a gain of equal magnitude.[7] Losses are extremely painful in the market and can quickly alter an overall plan. An example should help illustrate this. Imagine that you invested $1 million at the peak of the market. Your return over the next year was negative 50 percent. The following year, however, you have a great year as the market bounces back, and you earn 100 percent. What is your average annual return?

Most people would assume 25 percent over the two years. The problem is that your return is actually zero. The $1 million invested became $500,000 by the end of year one. You then made $500,000 in year two to return to the original amount. Losses, especially large ones, are detrimental to long-term results. The larger the loss,

---

7   Daniel Kahneman, *Thinking, Fast and Slow* (New York: Farrar, Straus and Giroux, 2011).

the exponentially larger the subsequent gain to break even.

Warren Buffett was on to something when he stated, "The first rule of investing is to not lose money. The second is to not forget the first rule." All G7 countries, seven of the most advanced economies as reported by the International Monetary Fund, have experienced at least one period where stocks have lost at least 75 percent of their value. The math of a 75 percent loss is daunting. If you lost 75 percent of your portfolio in a market decline, you would have to earn a 300 percent return to break even.[8] Therein lies the problem with traditional buy and hold investing. Obviously, where you start is essential to determining success rates.

The goal of our approach is to earn what the market earns with less risk. The old Wall Street adage, "If you take care of the downside, the upside will take care of itself," resonates with truth. We know that by cutting the risk of the market, we can live to fight another day. Furthermore, we understand that if we can use the appropriate process, we can average what the market averages and hopefully cut the risk in half. An investor must be equipped with the proper tools to be able to play offense or defense.

---

8 Mebane Faber and Eric Richardson, *The Ivy Portfolio: How to Invest Like the Top Endowments and Avoid Bear Markets* (New York: John Wiley & Sons, 2009).

To demonstrate the potential benefits of reducing portfolio risk, we decided to compare two different hypothetical strategies. The period we analyzed was from 1964 until 2014. One of the strategies is a low-risk portfolio, and the other is the S&P 500. The low risk strategy was made using a random number generator with the parameters of having the same arithmetic average return as the S&P 500 (11.50 percent) but with 50 percent less volatility. The end result is that the low-risk strategy has 70 percent more money at the end of the fifty-year period. You don't have to *beat* the market to deliver market-beating results. You only have to *be* the market and avoid making the big mistakes.

The key to avoiding the big declines is to have a way of measuring sentiment so as to avoid the extremes. In other words, when it is obvious that the market participants are extremely optimistic, it is most likely time to become pessimistic. By acting contrarily, the prudent investor will be able to avoid the eventual drop back to reality and seek opportunity in the midst of crowded distrust. Contrarian investing is easier said than done, however; and a disciplined process is required.

As early as twelve thousand years ago, the Blackfoot Indians practiced a communal hunting ritual called "pishkun". The tribe would scare herds of bison off of a cliff where they would break their legs. Other tribe members would be waiting at the bottom to finish the kill. The main goal of the tribe was to scare one bison enough to dive off the cliff because they knew the herd would follow. Often times a young brave tribe member would be used as a decoy to lead the bison to the edge of the cliff. Dressed in bison skins, the decoy would run to the edge of the cliff once the other tribe members attacked. This type of hunting was an efficient form of slaughter for the Native Americans. The herding nature of the bison ultimately led to their demise.

Going against the crowd, as in the case of the bison, can be a brave but worthwhile task. The problem is that fighting our innate herd mentality is difficult and according to neuro-scientists, painful. James Montier, author and investment strategist at GMO (Grantham, Mayo, Otterloo, LLC) makes reference to a social exclusion experiment in his book, *Behavioral Investing*. "Players think they are playing in a three-way game with two other players, throw-ing a ball back and forth. In fact, the two other players are computer controlled. After a period of three-way play, the other two 'players' began to exclude the participant by throwing the ball back and forth between themselves. This social exclusion generates brain activity in the anterior cingulate cortex and the insula, both of which are also activated by real physical pain." The experiment revealed something profound: the brain experiences social exclusion in the same way as excruciating pain. Since we are wired to avoid pain, it is obvious that we are also inclined to follow the crowd.

Herding is common in the market today. Investors often flock to the hottest idea or the most exciting market. Herd mentality creates the euphoria and the negativity that we often see in the marketplace. It is largely to blame for the presence of bubbles and busts evident in past market cycles. The root cause of herding is our short-term focus. In studies about delayed gratification, researchers find that most people will choose a smaller reward today versus a slightly larger reward in the future. Short-term focus is also a reason why people commit robberies and other financial crimes. The prospect of an immediate reward is given larger weight than the long-term consequences.

Investors need a disciplined, quantitative approach to avoid the manic-depressive moments of the masses. It is not as easy as seeing what the crowd is doing, and doing the opposite. Martin Pring, in his book *Investment Psychology Explained*, stated that investors are usually right, just not at extremes.[9] Therefore, investors should have an empirically proven method for accurately identifying these extremes.

---

9 Martin Pring, *Investment Psychology Explained* (New York: John Wiley & Sons, 1993).

Introducing The CAPE

The fundamental belief of value investing is that the market is mean reverting. Most human beings are preset to expect current conditions to continue. This bias is the failure to account for mean reversion. Mean reversion means that future outcomes are likely to be close to their historical average. In the US economy, profit margins are probably the most mean-reverting data set we observe. This should be expected, as huge profits tend to attract competitors, compressing margins. When we observe the data, we see that profit margins oscillate over a long period of time. Higher margins are followed by lower levels and vice versa. The US economy has enjoyed above average profit margins for the last four years. In fact, profit margins in the US are at the highest levels in the last sixty years. Nevertheless, financial analysts on Wall Street predict profit margins to continue to surge. Wall Street is failing to account for mean reversion.

Failing to account for mean reversion can harm results. As prices deviate from the intrinsic value, investors often fail to realize that the pendulum usually swings back. Positive deviation is usually a welcome experience by most investors. In fact, positive movement above an average is what usually attracts more people into the market, often creating euphoric excesses. This can often be disastrous as the crowd is usually wrong when sentiment is at extremes.

Extraordinary rises in prices are easy to identify in hindsight, giving us the overconfidence that we will be able to quickly recognize the next occurrence. During bubbles, irrationality is met with a new hysteria—the belief that "things are different this time."[10] In the market today, several market experts continue to make the case for higher stock prices despite the obvious overvalued conditions.

The goal of our approach is to capitalize on mass market psychology. Investors should profit from excessive optimism or pessimism and look at all sides of a belief before committing. "To be a contrarian, an investor must sell when the overall market mood is optimistic and buy when most investors are cynical."[11] How does one know when the overall market mood is optimistic or unenthusiastic? The key to gauging sentiment is to rely on long-term valuation.

Benjamin Graham believed in the importance of having a margin of safety before taking a position. "Value investing is the one form of investing that puts risk management at the very heart

---

10 Charles D. Kirkpatrick and Julie Dahlquist, *Technical Analysis: The Complete Resource for Financial Market Technicians* (Upper Saddle River, NJ: FT Press, 2010).

11 Kirkpatrick and Dahlquist, *Technical Analysis*.

of the approach."[12] Value investing is grounded in taking the contrarian stance, buying when others are selling, and selling when others are buying. Historically, value investing has generated above-average returns and is one of the common factors referred to in the Fama-French factor model. Why the outperformance? The efficient market enthusiasts would quickly cite risk as the culprit, stating that undervalued markets and stocks have higher risk. We disagree; we think the reason is behavioral.

When price exceeds intrinsic value by a large degree, sentiment has reached an extreme. If the fundamental value of the market is $100, but the price of the market is $200, then the psychology of the market participants is obviously optimistic. An overly enthusiastic investing public creates a market that is subject to disappointment. On the contrary, if the intrinsic value of the market is $100, but the price is $50, then the market participants are overly negative. Gloomy market participants allow for positive surprises. Quantitative valuation techniques provide us with the tools necessary to determine when the crowd is overly hopeful about the future or excessively negative.

There are several historically reliable methods to measure intrinsic value. When measuring

---

12   James Montier, *Value Investing: Tools and Techniques for Intelligent Investment* (West Sussex, England: John Wiley & Sons Ltd., 2009).

the underlying worth of a market, it is important that the investor does not rely on forecasts but instead on historical data. Behavioral finance argues that human beings are horrible at predicting the future. Therefore, we recommend staying clear of any measure that indicates forward-looking estimates are used. One example of this type of measurement is the forward price-to-earnings ratio[13]. Forward implies that the denominator is the estimate for next year's earnings. Since no one can predict what next year's earnings will be, this is a poor choice for measuring fundamental value.

Price-to-earnings ratios are the most widely referenced of all valuation ratios. The underlying assumption in the ratio is that the price of a stock or market should be directly related to the underlying profits. The proportion of price per share to earnings per share allows investors to compare various companies and markets to get an indication of whether a particular stock or market is expensive or inexpensive. Benjamin Graham, the father of value investing and Warren Buffett's mentor, recommended normalizing the price-to-earnings (P/E) ratio by taking an average of at least the last five years of earnings data. Hence, the normalized P/E ratio became known as the Graham and Dodd P/E. The notion of normalizing earnings makes sense in

---

13 Price-to-earnings ratio is the current price divided by either historical earnings per share or forecasted earnings per share.

that it levels out the effect any one year will have on the ratio. Using multiple years will give the investor a more reliable earnings measure to use when judging intrinsic value. The premise is that, over a longer period, profits revert to the average.

Robert Shiller uses the Graham and Dodd P/E, but instead of five years, he recommends using ten years of earnings data to normalize the ratio.[14] The Shiller method has become immensely popular and is known as the Shiller CAPE (cyclically adjusted price-to-earnings ratio). The idea is to use an average of earnings to measure fundamental value instead of wasting energy attempting to forecast future earnings.

A great deal of work has been done on the Shiller CAPE, highlighting the fact that lower CAPE values usually lead to higher average returns, and higher CAPE values lead to lower average returns (see Figure 2). That is what we want in a valuation indicator. It has merit if higher readings indicate that the market is too confident and thus poised for lower returns and vice versa. As far as the Shiller CAPE is concerned, the average since the late 1800s has been close to 16. Above 16, the market is considered overvalued, and below 16, the market is undervalued. The more extreme the CAPE value, the more noticeable the inverse relationship with subsequent long-term returns.

14   Robert Shiller, *Irrational Exuberance* (Princeton, NJ: Princeton University Press, 2000).

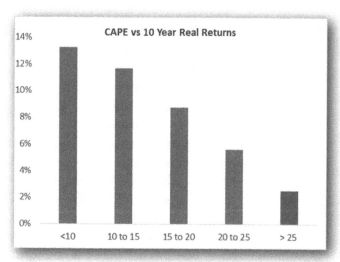

Figure 2: CAPE and 10 Year Returns
Source: Mebane Faber, CMT, CAIA

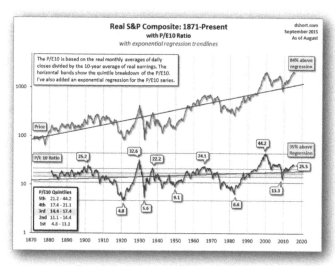

Figure 3: CAPE and the Stock Market
Source: Doug Short

The CAPE reverts to the mean over time, and the peaks and troughs of the indicator correlate with the peaks and troughs of the market (see Figure 3). When the CAPE has been high, historically large declines have resulted. Value investing is just as much about avoiding overvalued assets as it is about investing in undervalued ones. The CAPE provides a historically accurate tool for determining whether returns are going to be above average or below average over the long term.

The procedure we will show you can work with the CAPE ratio, the Q ratio, the market capitalization–to-GDP ratio, and several others. The point is to use historically reliable measures of intrinsic value to identify sentiment extremes. These extremes provide an opening for the savvy investor to position contrary to the herd.

History And The CAPE

To provide evidence in favor of the utility of the CAPE (cyclically adjusted price-to-earnings ratio), we will examine each of the past secular bull and bear markets since 1900, measuring the subsequent returns from related highs and lows in valuations.

1901-1921

The time period of 1901-1921 was critical in the history of the US and the World. In 1901, President

William McKinley became the third American president to be assassinated. Vice President Theodore Roosevelt replaced him at the age of 42, becoming the youngest President in history. The assassination of President McKinley marked the highpoint for the railroad stocks as Roosevelt's "Square Deal" promised to dismantle their dominance. The regime change at the beginning of the twentieth century marked the high point for valuations. In 1901, the stock market reached a CAPE level of over 25. Over the entire historical record of the CAPE, this is in the top quartile of values. The crowd was obviously extremely optimistic about the outlook in the United States during this period, and the sentiment was evident in valuations.

The overall market peaked five years after valuations peaked going nowhere for two decades. After inflation, the market plunged 69 percent from 1906 to 1921. There were several cyclical bull and bear markets during the time period. The first cyclical bear market occurred in 1907. Investors quickly pulled their money out of depository institutions in response to the fall in stock prices, indicating a heightened proclivity for cash. In 1907, J.P. Morgan had to broker a deal to prevent the bankruptcy of key financial institutions and save the financial system from collapse. After a rally from the 1907 lows, the stock market peaked in 1909 and moved sideways until the 1919-1921 deflationary bust.

In response to the financial distress of 1907, the Federal Reserve was created in November of 1914 under President Woodrow Wilson. The Wilson administration created the Fed to provide flexibility and an elastic currency to protect the banking system. Ironically, the US experienced inflationary pressures shortly after the Fed was created, as American industrial companies were producing the goods needed by the European militaries during the beginning of World War I.

The US entered World War I in April of 1917 and inflation continued to accelerate in the US. The war ended in 1918 and post war deflation soon hit. From 1919-1921 the dollar increased by over 60 percent against the Swiss franc and Deutsche mark. The increase in the US currency signified a deflationary trend and prices plunged.

The CAPE reached a low of 4.78 in late 1920 as prices became severely depressed. The drop in valuations was one of the most remarkable in market history. In fact, the 4.78 reading was the lowest CAPE value ever recorded in the US.

If an investor retired in 1901 and put all his money into the stock market for the next twenty years, he would have earned a horrible 0.61 percent return per annum. Those returns are awful compared to the 6.91 percent per year earned by the market from 1871 to 2014 (after inflation).

Prudent value investors should have been able to recognize the extreme level of sentiment by measuring the overvaluation. A well-designed system would have allowed investors to avoid buying the market at such levels and may have even prompted prudent investors to reduce their equity exposure.

1921-1929

If you had closed your eyes and bought the market in 1921, you would have realized a growth rate of 9.43 percent per year after inflation for the next twenty years. The returns are the same as compounding $1 into $6. From 1921 through the beginning of 1929, an investor would have earned an annual compound rate of return of over 25 percent.

The value investor should seek to buy when others are despondently selling. To reach a valuation of 4.78, the market was pricing in despair. The newly created Federal Reserve responded to deflation by raising the discount rate to 6 percent by 1920. This created the necessary capital inflow to put the economy and the market back onto solid footing. The result was a massive rally where shares of US corporations increased over 400 percent.

The advantage to value investing is that the astute investor is able to recognize a price that has deviated too far from intrinsic value and capitalize by buying the market. Buying and holding the index from low valuations can create attractive returns. Value allows you to invest in the market when probabilities suggest future growth.

The period from 1921-1929 became known as the "Roaring Twenties" as new technologies such as the radio, the automotive, and air flight ushered in an economic and cultural boom. An era of peace and prosperity was upon Americans and investors responded with a renewed sense of confidence. Stock investing became commonplace among many of the nation's households. Investors were even borrowing money to buy stocks, believing that the stock market only moved in one direction. In fact, nearly $4 of every $10 borrowed from the banks was used to buy stock in US companies. During the height of the bull market in 1929, the wealthiest 1 percent of Americans owned one-third of all assets.

1929-1932

The euphoria was evident by the overbought conditions in the market. The market continued to rally for part of the year in 1929, actually reaching a peak valuation of 32 in September of that year. The Federal Reserve raised interest rates several times in 1929 to cool the overheated stock market. The aggressive action by the Fed eventually created the top in the market and panic soon began.

The high valuations were an early warning sign of the coming destruction investors would face. The CAPE reached extremes in late 1928. If you would have bought the stock market at the beginning of 1929 and held it for twenty years, you would have barely earned over 1 percent per year. This is quite the departure from the 9 percent earned per annum if you bought in 1921. Even worse, the market declined from 1929 to 1932 by 81 percent. It would have been difficult to watch your account drop by 80 percent and continue to hold and hope.

The panic of 1929 marked the beginning of the Great Depression. The Fed was successful in cooling off the economy and bringing in a fresh bout of deflation. Economic activity collapsed, unemployment surged and the stock market entered another long secular bear market. Industrial production fell by over 47 percent, gross domestic product collapsed by 30 percent and wholesale prices dropped 33 percent. In 1932, the unemployment rate climbed above 20 percent and millions of people were left homeless. The destruction even spread to the elite where many lost everything in the stock market collapse.

1932-1937

The market collapse that occurred during the Great Depression was disastrous for investors. The

CAPE fell from a peak of 32 to below 10 at the end of 1931. If investors had bought the market when the market became extremely undervalued, they would have earned over 8 percent per year after inflation over the next twenty years. Over the shorter term, the market rallied 266 percent from the 1932 trough into the short-term peak in 1937. The CAPE was able to adequately pick up on the discrepancy between market price and fundamental reality.

As valuations dropped into the bottom quartile of historical observations, the CAPE was signaling that anyone who bought would be pleased over the long term. Buying and holding the market from 1932 would have been optimal in hindsight. Obviously, it would have been extremely difficult to buy during the despair of the Great Depression. The point is that following valuations can clue us in to the trajectory of future long-term returns.

The stock market rallied from 1932 to 1937 and then fell again. The CAPE was back above 20 by the start of 1937, once again signaling overly hopeful conditions. The market plummeted another 55 percent from 1937 to 1949. The economy suffered as the US entered another recession in 1937. The Federal Reserve, under political pressure to stave off potential inflation, tightened monetary policy in 1937. This caused gross domestic product to drop over 9 percent and industrial production to decline by over 40 percent. The premature move by the Federal Reserve plunged the US back into the grips of deflation.

Valuations reached their trough in 1942, ten years after the previous bottom. The CAPE was under 10 at the beginning of 1942, signaling a fearful market. The US had declared war on Japan in 1941 and wartime spending had resulted in a resurgence of economic activity.

1942-1962

If you had bought the market in 1942, you would have earned almost 13 percent (after inflation) over the next twenty years. Those returns are phenomenal and would have meant incredible compounding power over that twenty-year period. One dollar invested at the beginning of 1942 would have grown to over $11 by the end of 1961. The ability to quantitatively measure market sentiment would have helped investors capitalize on the Great Depression and position themselves for huge returns.

World War II ended in 1945 and the next twenty years were characterized by an expanding economy, swelling middle class, and a general rise in the price of stocks. Unemployment fell and all social classes grew wealthier. Military spending stayed rather buoyant as the Cold War (1947) and the Korean

War (1950) kept the military industrial complex at full throttle. Military and government spending were large contributors to economic growth.

In 1962, the market had been on a twenty-year tear, and valuations peaked at over 22. The market then transitioned into a sideways market over the next twenty years. An investor buying the market in 1962 would have earned less than 1 percent (0.78 percent), after accounting for inflation, through 1982.

The market actually peaked in 1968, showing the tendency for the CAPE to be early in signaling optimism. Imagine you sold your stocks when the market became extremely overvalued in 1962; you would have had to wait and watch an additional six years of market appreciation before finally reaching the highs. Despite the lack of timeliness, the CAPE was still able to pick up on the extreme euphoria and guide expectations.

1962-1982

The market peaked in 1968 and fell a whopping 63 percent before bottoming in 1982. Valuations plunged for twenty years, bottoming in 1982 with a CAPE value of less than 8. In 1982, the US economy was struggling in the midst of an almost twenty-year stagnation. High unemployment, low growth, and high inflation had a stranglehold on the US economy and the market.

The postwar economic expansion came to an end with the collapse of the Bretton Woods System in 1971. Nixon removed the US dollar from the gold standard and changed to a faith-based currency. The market crashed from 1973-1974 and inflation set in causing interest rates to soar. Paul Volker instituted tough decisions in the early 1980's in order to ease the inflationary pressures, pushing the US economy into recession. If you fought your better judgment and followed the CAPE, buying the market at the beginning of 1982, you would have earned monstrous returns over the next twenty years.

1982-2000

The market rallied over 600 percent from 1982 into the 2000 peak. A dollar invested in the market in 1982 would have compounded at 12 percent per year through 2002. Investors would have seen that dollar grow to over $9 during that period.

The invention of the internet created a gold rush in the United States. All of a sudden there was a new, untapped marketplace with unlimited potential. The internet would forever change the way business was conducted. New companies began to emerge and achieve astronomical growth. Investors took notice and stock prices surged.

Speculation in tech stocks was more about price momentum than the fundamentals of the companies themselves. In 1996, Federal Reserve Chairman Alan Greenspan warned against "irrational exuberance", noticing the widespread disconnect between valuations and market prices. The market continued to rally another four years after those famous words. Initial public offerings became rampant by the height of the bubble. Companies that had no revenue were doubling on their first day of trading in the open market. Investors were blinded by the early successes of internet companies and grew too excited about future prospects.

The market peaked in 2000 at a CAPE valuation of over 44. The technology bubble ushered in a period of extreme sentiment, whereby the CAPE reached extremes seven years prior to the ultimate peak. Nonetheless, the euphoria that gripped the market would ultimately cause the expiration. The "irrational exuberance" of market participants set up investors for a period where the market dropped a total of 55 percent during the subsequent nine years, bottoming in 2009. If you had bought the market in 2000, you would have achieved paltry returns of 1.91 percent per year through 2014.

2009-Today

The credit bubble came on the back of the Federal Reserve's aggressive monetary reaction to the decline in stock prices from the technology bust. The Federal Reserve lowered interest rates to 1 percent and flooded the market with easy money. It worked, temporarily. The easy money—combined with financial engineering—allowed a massive real estate bubble to form. Houses were being sold to individuals with no employment, no income, and no credit. The market was flush with cash as global investors were purchasing mortgage-backed bonds, searching for yield in an otherwise low-yield environment. The new demand created massive price increases in all asset classes. Bonds, stocks, commodities, and real estate surged on the back of the credit expansion.

The credit bubble came to an abrupt end as the housing market began to crack in 2006 and 2007. Defaults started to rise sharply, and soon banks were going under. The government had to step in and alter accounting rules, bail out many of the nation's largest financial institutions, and provide implicit and explicit guarantees to stop the panic. Housing prices were cut in half; global stocks fell by over 50 percent; and commodities (with the exception of gold and silver) dropped precipitously. The Chairman of the Federal Reserve, Ben Bernanke, stepped in and did what any sane person would do when an easy-money credit bubble bursts: he provided more easy money.

The collapse of Bear Stearns, Lehman Brothers, AIG, Wachovia, Countrywide, Merrill Lynch, and several other financial institutions created a massive panic unlike any experienced in the post–World War II era. Comparisons to the Great Depression surfaced, and the period was deemed the Great Recession.

The decline in asset prices came in a long-term, choppy fashion, with two separate declines of over 50 percent in 2000–2003 and in 2007–2009. The interesting thing is that valuations never reached below average during the first decline from 2000 to 2003. The CAPE stayed in the mid- to high twenties throughout the majority of the 2000s. It was not until the bottom in 2009 and the end of the credit bubble that the market finally reached low valuations.

Valuations dropped from over 44 in 2000 to bottom in March of 2009 at 13. If you were following the CAPE, you would have been clued in to the negative sentiment. The occasion to buy was present at the beginning of 2009 as valuations were back to earth, and the market had once again experienced a period of subpar returns. An investor who bought the market in 2009 would have achieved a compound annual growth rate of over 17 percent (after inflation) through the end of 2014.

We can only guess what returns will look like going forward from today. At the end of 2014, the CAPE stood at a lofty 27. History has shown this valuation level to be in the extremes of the distribution, placing it in the top 10 percent of valuations ever recorded. If the previous examinations provided anything, they demonstrated that buying when valuations are this high is often met with disappointment over the long term.

The obvious notion is that the market has historically peaked when valuations have indicated euphoria and troughed when investors were negative. Historical observations demonstrate that stretched valuations usually lead to secular tops and bottoms. Moreover, the historical record of the CAPE has demonstrated to us that the price we pay for an asset matters.

CHAPTER 2

Value Allocator System

Fisher and Statman (2006)[15], Smithers and Wright (2000)[16], and Stein and DeMuth (2003)[17] have all written about the merits of using valuation-based, market-timing strategies. All of these authors have demonstrated that using valuations (long-term valuations) to time the markets has historically yielded superior performance versus a buy-and-hold approach. Furthermore, the studies have concluded that the outperformance comes on the back of relatively low turnover and less risk than the standard set-it-and-forget-it philosophy of market investing.

Dr. Wade Pfau has written extensively about valuation-based approaches, demonstrating

15 Fisher and Statman, Market timing in regression and reality. *Journal of Financial Research* 2006 293-304

16 Smithers and Wright, *Valuing Wall Street: Protecting Wealth in Turbulent Markets.* New YorkMcGraw-Hill 2000

17 Stein and DeMuth, *Yes, You Can Time the Market.* Hoboken (John Wiley and Sons 2003)

the effectiveness of allocating assets based on long-term measures of value like the CAPE.[18] His methodology differed from the previously mentioned authors, as they all rotated from 100 percent stocks to 100 percent cash or fixed income based on whether the market was over- or undervalued. Dr. Pfau instead uses a model in which he allocates 50 percent to stocks and 50 percent to bonds unless the market is extremely overvalued (four-thirds of the rolling median) or extremely undervalued (two-thirds of the rolling median). If the market is extremely overvalued, the recommendation would be an allocation of 25 percent to stocks and 75 percent to bonds, and if undervalued, the weightings would be reversed. Dr. Pfau's papers demonstrated that his recommended methodology has histori-cally resulted in superior investment results and lower risk.

In the *Wall Street Journal* article "Yes, You Can Time the Market," Spencer Jakab gives readers a glimpse into the world of value-based asset allocation. He states that if investors had rebalanced[19] their balanced portfolios of 60 per-cent stocks and 40 percent bonds based on the

---

18 Pfau, Long-Term Investors and Valuation-Based Asset Allo-cation. *Applied Financial Economics* 2012

19 Rebalancing is the process of realigning assets in a portfolio as needed.

CAPE, the investors would have been much better off since 1926.

Lately there has been a great deal of criticism on the CAPE measure, with many critics viewing the metric as dated or no longer useful. Our opinion is that most of the doubts come from an erroneous application of a still useful tool. Specifically, most of the critics attempt to use the CAPE to time short-term market moves.

The basis of our value-allocation process is that we rebalance a portfolio based on where the CAPE value is at that point in time. For simplicity's sake, we are only going to examine the S&P 500 and US ten-year Treasury bond. We will assume you are an investor with a moderate risk tolerance and a long-term time horizon of greater than ten years. The appropriate benchmark will consist of half stocks and half bonds: 50 percent S&P 500 and 50 percent US ten-year Treasury bonds. The fifty-fifty allocation happens to be close to the average allocation in all of the valuation-based market-timing strategies we have referenced. Most money managers allocate according to the benchmark and then rebalance at some predetermined interval or drift. Drift is a term used to describe the deviation from the predetermined weighting. In a simplified version of our Value Allocator, we instead allow for flexibility in the portfolio, allocating based on the following rules:

- When the CAPE value is above the rolling thirty-year median, the portfolio will allocate 30 percent to the S&P 500 and 70 percent to US ten-year Treasuries.
- When the CAPE value is below the rolling thirty-year median, the portfolio will allocate 70 percent to the S&P 500 and 30 percent to US ten-year Treasuries.
- Each portfolio is rebalanced on an annual basis using the CAPE value as of December of the year before.

The test compares an investment of $1 million in a 50 percent S&P 500 and 50 percent US ten-year Treasury bond and $1 million invested in the Value Allocator beginning in 1928.[20] Through 2014, the balanced portfolio of half stocks and half bonds grew to an impressive $731,705,612.74. The balanced portfolio compounded at more than 7 percent per year over the entire period. The Value Allocator, on the other hand, grew to a whopping $1,188,715,737.16, compounding at roughly 9 percent and generating over $450 million more than the traditional portfolio (please see Figure 4).[21]

---

20 All testing is hypothetical and done with the benefit of hindsight. The data does not represent actual performance.

21 All calculations were made using www.econ.yale.edu/~shiller/data.htm and http://pages.stern.nyu.edu/~adamodar/New_Home_Page/datafile/histretSP.html.

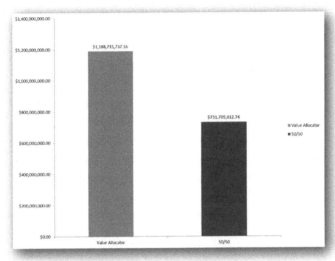

Figure 4: Value Allocator vs. Moderate Portfolio
(Growth of $1,000,000) 1928-2014

The difference in ending values is largely due to CAPE's ability to pick up extreme levels of sentiment. When markets are overvalued, sentiment is often euphoric. On the flip side, when markets are undervalued, sentiment is often pessimistic. The Value Allocator responds to the extremes in sentiment to rebalance the portfolio from a contrarian viewpoint. The strategy takes advantage of the irrational market participants by measuring when the market is overly optimistic or overly pessimistic and reacting accordingly.

Using value to determine the proper asset mix protects you from dangerous investor behavior, positioning you in a stance contrary to the masses. In addition, it protects against the market turmoil, as crashes are often associated with the times after extreme euphoria. Unlike static approaches to investment management, value-based asset allocation allows for adaptability. Charles Darwin stated, "It is not the strongest species that survives nor the most intelligent, but the one most responsive to change." The Value Allocator readily reacts to change in a fashion that is beneficial to the investor. Table 1 demonstrates the hypothetical performance data for our system, compared to a moderate benchmark of 50 percent stocks and 50 percent bonds.

To get a better picture of how our approach protects investors, we should examine the great bear markets of the past century. Let us look back upon how well the program would have worked during the Great Depression, the bear market of the 1970s, the technology bubble, and the most recent credit collapse.[22]

---

22 All data is hypothetical and calculated with the benefit of hindsight. The data does not represent actual performance.

Year	Value Allocator	50/50
1928	13.73%	22.33%
1929	0.45%	-2.05%
1930	-4.36%	-10.29%
1931	-14.94%	-23.20%
1932	-3.41%	0.08%
1933	35.54%	25.92%
1934	5.22%	3.39%
1935	34.06%	25.61%
1936	13.10%	18.48%
1937	-9.64%	-16.98%
1938	11.73%	16.75%
1939	2.76%	1.66%
1940	0.58%	-2.64%
1941	-5.25%	-7.40%
1942	14.11%	10.73%
1943	18.29%	13.78%
1944	14.10%	10.81%
1945	13.41%	19.81%
1946	-0.34%	-2.65%
1947	3.92%	3.06%
1948	4.58%	3.83%
1949	14.21%	11.48%
1950	21.70%	15.62%
1951	16.49%	11.69%
1952	7.03%	10.21%
1953	2.54%	1.47%
1954	37.78%	27.93%

1955	8.84%	15.63%
1956	0.65%	2.59%
1957	1.62%	-1.83%
1958	11.65%	20.81%
1959	1.76%	4.71%
1960	8.25%	5.99%
1961	9.43%	14.35%
1962	1.34%	-1.56%
1963	7.96%	12.15%
1964	7.54%	10.08%
1965	4.22%	6.56%
1966	-0.95%	-3.53%
1967	6.03%	11.11%
1968	5.53%	7.04%
1969	-5.98%	-6.63%
1970	12.79%	10.16%
1971	11.12%	12.01%
1972	7.60%	10.79%
1973	-1.73%	-5.33%
1974	-17.53%	-11.96%
1975	26.98%	20.31%
1976	21.48%	19.91%
1977	-4.50%	-2.85%
1978	4.32%	2.87%
1979	13.17%	9.60%
1980	21.32%	14.38%
1981	-0.83%	1.75%
1982	24.14%	26.62%
1983	16.60%	12.77%

1984	8.42%	9.94%
1985	29.58%	28.48%
1986	20.23%	21.39%
1987	2.58%	0.43%
1988	14.04%	12.38%
1989	27.34%	24.59%
1990	3.45%	1.59%
1991	19.57%	22.62%
1992	8.80%	8.43%
1993	12.94%	12.09%
1994	-5.23%	-3.36%
1995	27.60%	30.34%
1996	7.81%	12.06%
1997	16.89%	21.52%
1998	18.95%	21.63%
1999	0.49%	6.32%
2000	8.95%	3.82%
2001	0.34%	-3.14%
2002	3.99%	-3.43%
2003	8.77%	14.37%
2004	6.37%	7.62%
2005	3.46%	3.85%
2006	6.06%	8.79%
2007	8.79%	7.85%
2008	3.11%	-8.23%
2009	14.82%	7.41%
2010	12.91%	11.64%
2011	11.86%	9.07%
2012	12.01%	9.43%

| 2013 | 3.28% | 11.53% |
| 2014 | 11.57% | 12.12% |

Table 1: Year by Year data for the Value Allocator

The Great Depression

In the historical data, the worst economic period was during the Great Depression in the early 1930s. Valuations became stretched at the end of 1928, and the system indicated a hypothetical rotation to a conservative portfolio construction of 30 percent stocks and 70 percent bonds. The market started the decline in 1929, dropping 8 percent. The slump continued as stocks declined 25 percent in 1930, 44 percent in 1931, and 8 percent in 1932. From 1929 until 1932, the S&P 500 fell over 80 percent— the greatest decline in US stock market history.

The Value Allocator, because of the conservative positioning, was flat in 1929 and down 4 percent in 1930, 15 in 1931, and 3 percent in 1932. Hypothetically, the system would have successfully protected investors against a horrific decline. The ability to pick up on the extreme sentiment at the end of 1928 allowed for the flexibility to limit exposure to the market during 1929 and 1930. After a rally from 1932 to 1937, the market once again reached an overbought extreme and fell 35 percent in 1937. The market continued to muddle along until finally bottoming in 1942.

Our process would have once again picked up on the overbought condition of the S&P 500. The recommended allocation going into 1937 was 30 percent stocks and 70 percent bonds. The result was a decline of only 10 percent. The system would have clearly protected investors against another large decline.

The Bear Market of 1962–1982

In 1973, the S&P 500 fell 14 percent and in 1974 declined an additional 26 percent. The period from 1962 to 1982 was characterized as a period of stagflation where the economy was gripped by stagnant growth, high inflation, and high unemployment. After accounting for inflation, the market plummeted over 60 percent during this time. It would have taken investors a number of years to finally break even if they would have bought and held the S&P 500 in 1966, let alone 1973. However, if you had allocated assets according to the Value Allocator, you would have first rotated to a conservative portfolio in 1962 and would not have become aggressive again until 1974.

In 1973, the Value Allocator was down 2 percent and in 1974 down 17 percent. The system did a wonderful job protecting against the market declines and would have allowed investors the chance to position themselves well in the coming bull market of 1982–2000.

The "Dot-Com" Bubble

The Value Allocator is used to steer investors away from the crowded extremes. The system is often extremely early, and investors should be aware of this weakness. In the late 1990s, you would have shifted to a conservative asset allocation in 1990. The market rallied for another ten years. Not only did the market rally, but if you had invested $1 in the S&P 500 in January 1990, it would have been worth $4 by January 2000 (after inflation). Applying valuations may be simple, but going against the crowd is not easy.

Imagine you are at a cocktail party in 1998 during the heat of the technology bubble. Your friends are all bragging about their latest market conquests. Then the moment you have been trying to avoid surfaces when someone turns to you and asks, "How are your investments doing?" You have difficulty swallowing as you conjure up a way to frame your conservative stance without being laughed out of the party.

Then you say it: "I am currently only 30 percent in stocks and 70 percent in bonds." The chuckles begin.

"What is a bond?" you hear someone ask. Then the conversation gets deeper. "Why are you not invested?"

Then you commit the ultimate crime. Without thinking, you respond with, "The market is over-valued." You can now hear a pin drop as you have just insulted everyone engaged in the conversation.

Your friends reply in a defensive tone, "What about the Internet? The new economy? It is a new era!"

We think you get the picture. You may begin to question your strategy and wonder if it is still viable in today's world. Remember, social exclusion is painful.

Jeremy Grantham, one of the heads of GMO, lived through this experience, and it cost him big-time. GMO is a global investment management firm that currently manages $120 billion in client assets. During the late 1990s, he was warning of stretched valuations and was even predicting negative real returns for the stock market over the next ten years. His contrarian stance, based on a similar value approach, sent shock waves through the company as clients began to leave GMO in droves. It is rumored that GMO lost close to 50 percent of their business during this time. Keynes once opined that "markets can stay irrational longer than you can remain solvent." The irrationality of the market even made it difficult for the highly esteemed Jeremy Grantham.

Luckily, value is a long-term metric. By 2003, GMO had gained a plethora of business, having successfully navigated the dot-com bubble that sent the S&P 500 down over 50 percent from 2000 through 2003. Value investing shows its merit most when the markets decline. The margin of safety produced by buying when the market is undervalued and, most importantly, avoiding overvalued assets allows one to win by not losing.

If you had followed the Value Allocator, you would have totally sidestepped the end of the bubble. In the year 2000, the S&P 500 was down 9 percent. The Value Allocator was up 9 percent. In 2001, the S&P 500 was down 11.85 percent while the Value Allocator was up 0.34 percent. In 2002, the S&P 500 was down 21.97 percent while the Value Allocator was up 4 percent.

The pain of missing out on the rapid rise in stock prices during the late 1990s was made up for by the protection of principal achieved during the market turmoil. Protecting capital allows the investor to be positioned opportunistically when the market turns around.

The Credit Crisis

The late 1990s and the 2000s were some of the most interesting periods in market history. Valuations reached extremes in 1993 and stayed extreme until 2009. During the period from 2000 to 2009, the market experienced two bubbles and subsequent crashes.

From October 2007 through March 2009, the S&P 500 was cut by 55 percent. Investors' assets were cut in half for the second time in less than ten years. In 2008, the market declined 37 percent for the year. As with all the other market drops we have referenced, the Value Allocator protected the portfolio, finishing the year up 3 percent.

Fast forward now and imagine yourself at another cocktail party. This time it is March 2009, and you are with the same group of friends. Most likely, you are the only one with a remnant of a smile on your face. You have been following the Value Allocator since the 1990s, and you have successfully navigated both the technology collapse and the Great Recession. Everyone is depressed—their accounts have been cut in half twice, and they have been flat, too, over the last decade. Your friends now look at you as a genius. Your discipline has done the most important job: it has protected you against the certainty of market declines and helped you avoid making the big mistakes.

What about the Upside?

You are probably wondering what the catch is. There has to be some sort of price to be paid. Financial theory would have you believe that if the system has less risk than the market, then you must be sacrificing the growth. Fortunately, financial theory lacks practicality. Euphoria is often a sign that the market has run too far to the upside, and extreme doubt is a sign of an oversold market. The pessimistic side of market psychology is the most dramatic. Panic sets in and investors sell despondently. To borrow a saying of Warren Buffett, our system is designed to "buy when others are fearful." The CAPE does a good job at clueing us in to when the crowd is too fearful.

During the Great Depression, the market became dramatically oversold. Investors were fleeing stocks as quickly as they could, and by 1931 the market was extremely undervalued. If you had been investing according to the value-allocation methodology during that period, you would have shifted your allocation from 30 percent stocks and 70 percent Treasury bonds to 70 percent stocks and 30 percent Treasury bonds. With overvalued markets, the system has demonstrated the propensity to be early. It often recommends a conservative allocation long before the ultimate peak in price. When markets are undervalued, the system is also early, sometimes painfully so.

So 1932 was not a good year for the stock market as it declined roughly 9 percent. If you were following the Value Allocator, you would have been 70 percent in the market and experienced a decline of 3 percent. Remember that this is after the market tumbled 44 percent the year before. It would have been extremely difficult to increase exposure to the market during this time. If you followed the program, however, the Value Allocator would have set you up for the rebound that took place from 1932 to 1937. The market rallied 266 percent from the low in 1932 to the high of 1937. Protection is great, but protection and growth is even better. Having moved aggressively in 1932, the Value Allocator would have captured a majority of the rally. The returns and stock weightings are as follows:

    1932: −3.41% (70%)
    1933: 35.54% (70%)
    1934: 5.22% (30%)
    1935: 34.06% (70%)
    1936: 13.10% (30%)
    1937: −9.64% (30%)

The Value Allocator would have positioned a portfolio into a higher stock allocation from 1932 to 1936. 1934 was the only year when the system rotated back defensively, following a big growth year in 1933. The market became overvalued again in 1936 when the portfolio would have been allocated more conservatively (30 percent stocks).

The market eventually bottomed in 1942, during the middle of World War II. The Value Allocator once again picked up on the extreme crowd behavior and positioned 70 percent into stocks. The Value Allocator maintained 70 percent in stocks for eight of the next ten years. The benefit was that it would have allowed investors to capitalize on the massive recovery achieved by the stock market.

The actions of the Federal Reserve in the wake of the dot-com collapse temporarily prevented a much-needed mean reversion of valuations. The market was the most overbought in its entire history and stayed extremely overvalued until 2009. Even though the market corrected 50 percent from 2000 to 2003, valuations stayed above average. The Value Allocator would have never adjusted to the collapse of the stock prices in 2003 and would have stayed conservatively positioned until 2009. From 2003 to 2009, the Value Allocator portfolio would have trailed the fifty-fifty benchmark in four out of the seven years. The system largely missed out on the stock price appreciation in 2003–2007.

In 2009, the Value Allocator would have positioned 70 percent back into the stock market.

Once again, the Value Allocator would have allowed investors the chance to capture a majority of the market growth from a major bottom. The returns during the credit crisis are as follows:

	S&P 500	VA	50/50
2008	(36.55%)	3.11%	(8.23%)
2009	25.94%	14.82%	7.41%
2010	14.82%	12.91%	11.64%
2011	2.10%	11.86%	9.07%
2012	15.89%	12.01%	9.43%
2013	32.15%	3.28%	11.53%
2014	13.48%	11.57%	12.12%

From 2008 through 2014, the Value Allocator would have outperformed the benchmark allocation in five of the seven years. More importantly, the system would have grown in all seven years. The Value Allocator does a splendid job at capturing the fear in the market and reacting to position the portfolio properly for growth. The problem is that it is often painfully early and requires an immense amount of fortitude and discipline to stick with it. The Value Allocator is long-term by design, as it relies on mean reversion—a phenomenon best observed over periods greater than seven years. Investor behavior tells us that long-term strategies are extremely difficult to follow because of the short-term focus of market participants. Thus, creating a pragmatic program requires an additional layer.

CHAPTER 3

Tactical Asset Allocation

Trend following is using price to determine the appropriate allocation.[23] Price works as the ultimate indicator because of supply and demand. The irrefutable law of supply and demand has been the ultimate guide to navigating markets for centuries. Supply and demand governs how prices move. Therefore, price tells the true story. For instance, if there are more buyers than sellers, prices will rise. If there are more sellers than buyers, prices will fall.[24] Understanding what force is governing the market is critical to making allocation decisions. If supply is in control, you will want to avoid that market. On the other hand, you will want to invest in a market where demand is the stronger force.

23 Momentum and trend following will be used interchangeably. The system we demonstrate buys what is going up and sells what is going down.

24 Thomas J. Dorsey, *Point and Figure Charting: The Essential Application for Forecasting and Tracking Market Prices*, Third Edition (Hoboken, NJ: John Wiley & Sons, 2007).

Trend following is about maintaining a harmonious relationship with the market. The idea is that the market is the sum total of all the investment experience and expertise of the market participants. The collective knowledge of the group is, in theory, superior to the individual's over the long term. It is better to exist within a synchronous association rather than in opposition. According to a trend follower, "Mr. Market" is always right, no matter how seemingly irrational.

Trend following strategies have delivered superior performance to buy-and-hold investing.[25] Meb Faber used a simple moving-average procedure to allocate to the S&P 500 or cash, demonstrating that he could reduce the correlation of his strategy to the S&P 500 in the down markets to -0.38 and maintain a positive correlation of 0.83 during positive years.[26] Correlation is a measure to determine how assets move in relation to one another: plus one is a perfect positive correlation, meaning the assets move together; zero implies the assets do not move together and have unrelated activity; negative one is a perfect negative correlation, suggesting that assets move opposite from one another.

The implications of this study are profound. They indicate that by using a simple trend following methodology, one can create a scheme to reduce

25 Adam L. Berger, Ronen Israel, and Tobias J. Moskowitz, *The Cases for Momentum Investing* (Greenwich, CT: AQR, 2009).
26 Faber and Richardson, *The Ivy Portfolio*.

correlation to equities when most other correlations are rising. When correlations rise during periods of market uncertainty, portfolio risk increases. Faber provides a simple solution to this particular conundrum despite using the S&P 500 as the investment vehicle. Momentum and trend following are strategies used to diversify a portfolio and cut market risk through the avoidance of large slumps. [27]

We use trend following in order to take advantage of positive herd mentality and avoid negative herd mentality. We alternate between risk-on and risk-off, depending on the price trend of stocks and bonds. Capitalizing on herd mentality allows the investor to gain access to a return stream that does not always move in tandem with stocks and bonds. For example, during the time period from 2007 to 2009, the stock market (S&P 500) collapsed over 55 percent. Many managed-futures managers or commodity-trading advisors (CTAs) showed positive returns. Managed-futures managers are largely trend followers. Consequently, the managed-futures traders were negatively correlated with stocks and provided the ultimate diversification to a traditional portfolio. The time period from 2007 to 2009 is not unique. During several other market declines and reductions in

27 A simple moving average is the average price over a predefined time period. The average is moving in that it adjusts to new data by dropping off the oldest price and adding the newest price. Meb Faber illustrates a system using a 10 month simple moving average.

traditional asset classes, trend following traders demonstrated the ability to take advantage of the scrambling herd and capture impressive gains.

Trend following seems high risk to many investors who still look at risk as volatility. Many trend trading systems actually have higher volatility than the market. The fact is that volatility is not risk, and "the acceptance of higher risk in a trend following investment can actually lower the risk of your stock and bond portfolios because when trend following zigs, typical stock and bond investments zag."[28] Trend following appears to be an elixir for the behavioral ills of investing. Herd mentality, overconfidence, representativeness, anchoring effects, and loss aversion are all dealt with through systematic trend following, or momentum investing.

We can use simple rules to replicate a strategy that protects during market declines without sacrificing the upside. In our strategy, we use indices (baskets of securities tracking a particular market) to gain exposure because of their relatively low costs and high transparency. To illustrate the effectiveness of trend following historically, we are going to provide a simple, rules-based tactical allocation system as a model. The rules are as follows:[29]

---

28   Covel, *Trend Following*.

29   The calculations were made using Global Financial Data index data for the Russell 2000 Small Cap Index, S&P 500 index, and US ten-year Treasury bond index until 2003. After 2003, ETF data were used to better replicate an investable index. The following ETFs were used: IWM (Small Cap Stocks), SPY (S&P 500), IEF (ten-year Treasury bonds).

1. Rank the S&P 500, Russell 2000, and the US ten-year Treasury bond based on the three-month performance.
2. Pick the strongest index based on the ranking.
3. Run the ranking system each month.

The important information to gather from the historical results is the performance of the tactical strategy during the years when the market declines. The ability to rotate away from the stock market when the price deteriorates allows for better performance when trouble is present. The core tenet of trend following and momentum investing is the protection of capital. Hence, the tactical strategy would have demonstrated the most significant outperformance during periods in which the overall stock market is experiencing large declines.[30]

The strategy would have performed well during positive stock market environments. The portfolio can be invested in the stock market when the trend is positive and stocks are stronger than bonds. In other words, the simple trend trading system acts as a risk reducer during the down markets without sacrificing profits during up markets.

Our tactical strategy would have done well compared to the S&P 500 since 1972. In Figure

---

30 All data is hypothetical and calculated with the benefit of hindsight. The data does not reflect actual performance.

5, we illustrate the hypothetical results to better demonstrate the potential benefits of incorporating trend following. If you had invested $1 million in the S&P 500 in the beginning of 1972, your investment would have grown to over $72 million by the end of 2014. If you had invested your $1 million during the same period using our tactical strategy, it would have grown to over $335 million. Remember that the model can only maximize returns up to what the market earns. The potential outperformance comes from avoiding the down markets.

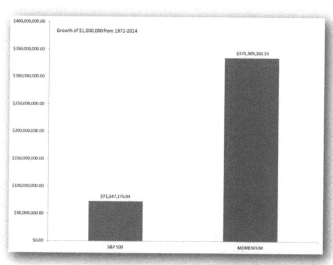

Figure 5: Trend following vs. S&P 500
(Growth of $1,000,000) 1972-2014

	S&P 500	Trend System
1972	18.8%	12.5%
1973	-14.3%	-2.0%
1974	-25.9%	-0.8%
1975	37.0%	37.6%
1976	23.8%	31.5%
1977	-7.0%	3.1%
1978	6.5%	0.7%
1979	18.5%	24.2%
1980	31.7%	22.5%
1981	-4.7%	6.9%
1982	20.4%	46.0%
1983	22.3%	27.8%
1984	6.2%	-2.2%
1985	31.2%	17.2%
1986	18.5%	17.3%
1987	5.8%	5.5%
1988	16.5%	22.3%
1989	31.5%	19.7%
1990	-3.1%	2.4%
1991	30.2%	36.1%
1992	7.5%	13.7%
1993	10.0%	6.6%
1994	1.3%	-4.7%
1995	37.2%	30.0%
1996	22.7%	15.0%
1997	33.1%	37.2%
1998	28.3%	29.1%

1999	20.9%	16.3%
2000	-9.0%	5.1%
2001	-11.9%	-6.4%
2002	-22.0%	-5.8%
2003	28.4%	39.8%
2004	10.7%	12.2%
2005	4.8%	1.3%
2006	15.6%	13.5%
2007	5.5%	-4.7%
2008	-36.6%	14.8%
2009	25.9%	21.1%
2010	14.8%	33.2%
2011	2.1%	17.4%
2012	15.9%	2.5%
2013	32.2%	35.9%
2014	13.5%	8.3%

Table 2: Trend Following vs. S&P 500

The tactical system does not avoid declines. Since the end of 1971, there have been nine years in which the S&P 500 declined. Over the past forty years, the trend trading strategy declined seven times (see Table 2). The beauty of trend following lies in avoiding the *big* declines. The strategy never suffered a loss of greater than 7 percent in any given year. In comparison, the market suffered five declines over 10 percent, of which three were over 20 percent. Investors must minimize the big declines to succeed when investing. The tactical system is able to accomplish the task of protecting the investors during big market declines, helping the portfolio grow more over the long term.

As we have outlined previously, trend following has historically worked to participate in up markets and protect against deep market declines. While we cannot predict the future trajectory of prices, we know that markets will fluctuate, and we have designed portfolios to potentially take advantage of market volatility. Trend following traders have demonstrated their ability to navigate the uncertain markets and capitalize on turmoil. Trend following is reserved not only for the Wall Street elite or the ultrarich. You can apply the same principles to diversify your portfolio using simple index funds.

CHAPTER 4

Putting It All Together

The Value Allocator is a robust enough program on its own to help you navigate the uncertain markets and avoid getting caught in the next crash. The problem is that the system is almost behaviorally impossible to apply. Using trend following as a method for tactical asset allocation is an important enhancement that will generate a pleasant investment experience.

The tactical strategy appears to deliver the best results within the illustration. However, we did not examine the impact of transaction costs (most likely negligible) and taxes (significant). We have no way to estimate the tax ramifications as it is obviously only successfully analyzed at the individual level. Trend following, because of the short-term gains, is most likely the least tax efficient.

Trend trading is difficult to follow year in and year out. Trend following does not always resemble the overall stock market. In fact, these types of strategies often look much different from the traditional stock indices such as the Dow Jones Industrial or the S&P 500. Individual investors often anchor themselves to the performance of these indices, regardless of how appropriate. The S&P 500 may not be the right comparative benchmark for a long-term investor with a conservative risk tolerance. Nevertheless, investors may abandon an approach that strays too far from the performance of the popular indices.

Since the bottom in 2009, the Barclays CTA Index (a common benchmark for trend following) has been down in every year except for 2010 and 2014. The stock market has not had a negative year since 2008. Again, trend strategies in isolation are extremely difficult to follow over a long period. In efforts to remain pragmatic, we have combined the Value Allocator and trend following to provide a comprehensive approach.

The combination of the two strategies keeps an investor from moving the entire portfolio tactically and keeps a portion in a strategic posture. Tactical asset allocation is the practice of taking positions in various investments based on short- to intermediate-term prospects. Our strategic asset allocation methodology is based on valuations and expected mean reversion. The problem is that mean reversion occurs over a period of seven to ten years. Valuations tell us very little about what is going to happen over the subsequent one to three years.

Our tactical overlay is therefore based on reacting to the trend. This is an interesting relationship, as the two strategies can offer up diametrically opposed recommendations. For instance, when the US stock market is overvalued, the Value Allocator would recommend rotating to a more conservative portfolio. At the same time, if the trend is positive, the tactical overlay would recommend overweighting equities. You can see the conflicts that can arise, and we assure you they have surfaced in the past.

An investor must be able to stick with their investment plan in order to achieve success and reach their financial goals. The conflict between the two systems is exactly what is needed. Choosing the right proportion of strategic versus tactical is critical to establishing the proper policy. Determining how much of your portfolio should be in the tactical portion of the portfolio is a decision based on your personal circumstances. You must ensure that you are comfortable with the range of exposure to each asset class. If you are uncomfortable, the purpose of providing a more palatable experience is defeated.

Ideally, the tactical portion of the portfolio should be determined by first deciding the minimum amount of risky assets the investor can handle. How do you determine what percentage of stocks you are comfortable with? We suggest taking a deep look inside and determining what loss you can withstand before you pull the plug on the investment program. The goal is to invest in a way that will keep you engaged in the markets and prevent emotional decision-making. The emotional breaking point is what you should be after. We know the market has declined over 50 percent twice in the last fifteen years. That is as good of a place as any to start thinking about your portfolio's risk. We suggest you start thinking about how you would react if the equity portion of the portfolio were cut in half. In the past, when the market has reached the valuation level that it is currently, it has stumbled significantly.

We strongly believe in addressing your individual objectives and constraints before deciding upon an appropriate methodology. Our routine is unique in that we allow the market to play a strong role in determining the risk tolerance. If the odds of higher returns are above average, we suggest allowing the portfolio to capitalize. Moreover, if the odds of below-average returns are high, we advocate moving defensively. The belief that an investor must decide on a risk tolerance without consulting the current market environment is illogical.

The Value Allocator—as illustrated for a moderate risk tolerance—can rotate between 30 percent stocks and 70 percent bonds and 70 percent stocks and 30 percent bonds. The tactical portfolio is either 100 percent in stocks or 100 percent in US ten-year Treasury bonds. The following matrix embodies all possible allocations when half of the portfolio is constructed according to the Value

Allocator and the other half is based on the tactical program.

	Undervalued Market	Overvalued Market
Positive Trend	85% stocks /15% bonds	65% stocks/35% bonds
Negative Trend	35% stocks /65% bonds	15% stocks /85% bonds

In our model, the investor can have as little as 15 percent in stocks and as much as 85 percent. The wide range allows the investor to adapt to all market conditions, protecting when the odds are poor and growing when the odds favor return enhancement. Instead of fixing the allocation on a static portfolio, investors are allowed the flexibility to adapt their risk tolerance to the current environment. For instance, if the current market environment is undervalued, and the trend is positive, the environment is favorable for stocks. Thus, the investor would be positioned heavily in that asset class.

We need to clarify the fact that just because the investor is overweight in stocks does not mean this cannot be remedied. As John Maynard Keynes said, "When the facts change, I change my mind. What do you do, Sir?" An intelligent investor is flexible enough to adapt to changing facts and position the portfolio appropriately.

Just because markets become overvalued, does not mean that they are going to crash immediately. In fact, the opposite is often true. Markets can become overvalued only to continue to rally for several years before finally peaking. Our discussion of the dot-com bubble highlighted this phenomenon best. Following only the Value Allocator would have had you underweight equities and underperforming the benchmark for a long period. Most likely, that would have been too painful to see through. The tactical portion of the portfolio would have allowed you to participate in more upside. For the most part, the tactical overlay would have generated market-like returns from 1990 through 2000 and sidestepped the market crash of 2000. In our illustration, the investor would have had 65 percent in stocks for most of the 1990s, despite the overvaluation.

Undervalued markets can be dangerous despite the favorable outlook. Value investors are often notoriously early and wrong for a time. The tactical portfolio allows for a more defensive posture in an undervalued market where an investor would hold 35 percent in stocks if the trend was down. Examining the 1973–1975 bear market may help shed some light. The market became undervalued at the end of 1973, after the market declined 15 percent that year. If you were following the Value Allocator in isolation, you would have then rotated to 70 percent stocks from 30 percent stocks, getting aggressive just in time for a 26 percent drop in the market in 1974. The point is to protect investors—not set them up for a collapse.

The complementary tactical overlay allows investors to be early without being overly penalized. In our illustration, you would have had only 35 percent in stocks because the trend in the market was negative. More importantly, when the trend eventually turned positive, you would be prepared to shift 85 percent of the portfolio into stocks in order to capitalize on the low valuations and newfound positive trend. The combination is obviously beneficial as illustrated in Figure 6.

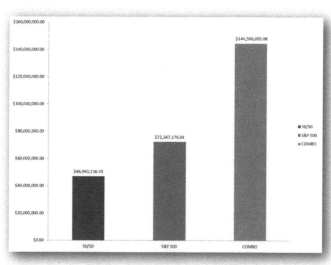

Figure 6: Combining Value and
Trend Following 1972-2014

The combination of the Value Allocator and tactical allocation strategy outpaced the S&P 500 and fifty-fifty benchmarks by a large degree.[31] The advantage of the combination of these two strategies is quite clear. The worst loss the combination strategy experienced from 1972 to 2014 was 9 percent in 1974 when the market was down almost 26 percent. The Value Allocator, when analyzed in isolation, was down almost 18 percent during that same year. The tactical plan would have added an extra layer of protection when the Value Allocator arrived early to the party. In addition to providing an extra layer of protection, the combination strategy could have provided growth that would have otherwise been missed during the late 1990s and from 2003 to 2007.

The market stayed overvalued from 1990 until the beginning of 2009. If you had followed the Value Allocator during this period, you would have been disappointed. The combination strategy would have minimized the underperformance to the benchmark by keeping you at a higher equity position throughout the 1990s. In Figure 7, you can see the market outperform the combination strategy over this period.

---

31 All data is hypothetical and calculated with the benefit of hindsight. The data does not reflect actual performance.

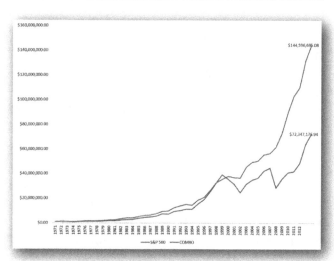

Figure 7: Combination vs. S&P 500 1972-2014

	S&P 500	Combination	50/50
1972	18.76%	10.07%	10.79%
1973	-14.31%	-1.86%	-5.33%
1974	-25.90%	-9.19%	-11.96%
1975	37.00%	32.31%	20.31%
1976	23.83%	26.47%	19.91%
1977	-6.98%	-0.69%	-2.85%
1978	6.51%	2.51%	2.87%
1979	18.52%	18.66%	9.60%
1980	31.74%	21.91%	14.38%
1981	-4.70%	3.01%	1.75%
1982	20.42%	35.09%	26.62%
1983	22.34%	22.21%	12.77%

1984	6.15%	3.10%	9.94%
1985	31.24%	23.38%	28.48%
1986	18.49%	18.76%	21.39%
1987	5.81%	4.02%	0.43%
1988	16.54%	18.19%	12.38%
1989	31.48%	23.54%	24.59%
1990	-3.06%	2.93%	1.59%
1991	30.23%	27.84%	22.62%
1992	7.49%	11.24%	8.43%
1993	9.97%	9.77%	12.09%
1994	1.33%	-4.97%	-3.36%
1995	37.20%	28.79%	30.34%
1996	22.68%	11.40%	12.06%
1997	33.10%	27.02%	21.52%
1998	28.34%	24.03%	21.63%
1999	20.89%	8.42%	6.32%
2000	-9.03%	7.04%	3.82%
2001	-11.85%	-3.01%	-3.14%
2002	-21.97%	-0.90%	-3.43%
2003	28.36%	24.29%	14.37%
2004	10.74%	9.28%	7.62%
2005	4.83%	2.38%	3.85%
2006	15.61%	9.78%	8.79%
2007	5.48%	2.05%	7.85%
2008	-36.55%	8.95%	-8.23%
2009	25.94%	17.96%	7.41%
2010	14.82%	23.06%	11.64%
2011	2.10%	14.63%	9.07%
2012	15.89%	7.26%	9.43%

| 2013 | 32.15% | 19.59% | 11.53% |
| 2014 | 13.48% | 9.93% | 12.12% |

Table 3: Combination Strategy

The market outperformance was only temporary, however, as the 50 percent decline from the peak in 2000 was largely avoided (see Table 3). In addition, instead of keeping the allocation conservative from 2003 to 2007, tactical positioning kept investors engaged in the markets. Following the Value Allocator alone from 2003 to 2007 would have had the investors conservatively positioned in 30 percent stocks and 70 percent bonds—largely missing the rebound from the tech wreck. The tactical component of the portfolio would have allowed investors to maintain 65 percent in stocks when the trend was positive, despite the overvalued conditions of the market.

Astute investors should diversify their strategic asset allocation with tactical positions. Value and momentum are two of the strongest factors of market returns, and their significance remains rather stable over time. Combining both value and momentum strategies in a disciplined fashion can create desirable results.

The strategic portion of our method is designed to be contrary to the herd. The purpose of this component of the portfolio is to avoid the crowded extremes. The issue is that you can't time the market, and following a value discipline often means you are early and wrong. Combining tactical asset allocation with the contrarian guidelines provides a complementary tool for protecting and growing your portfolio.

In market timing, you must be right more than you are wrong to make money. One wrong move and your portfolio can experience disastrous results. Too many investors try to time the market. They get swept into the emotions of the moment, and they lose sight of the long term. We are suggesting that you use a rules-based approach for this reason: *to avoid destructive behavior through emotional decision-making.* The combination strategy provides enough leeway for being wrong while enhancing the odds of achieving investment success.

CHAPTER 5

Enhancements

Going Global

We have demonstrated the effectiveness of using the CAPE (cyclically adjusted price-to-earnings ratio) to measure the value of the overall market. The CAPE has historically been a reliable guide of overall market sentiment, warning of euphoria and indicating when we are in the midst of pessimism. We have only focused on the US stock market in our examination due to the fact that we are US-domiciled investors, falling victim to *home bias*.

Home bias is when investors allocate too much of their assets to their own country. In our case, we would be biased if we put too much of our portfolio in the US markets. A 2012 Vanguard study looked at home bias in investor portfolios since 2001. The findings were quite interesting in that US investors, on average, held about 29 percent more US stocks than the US share of global market capitalization.

The study examines data through 2010, when the US share of global market capitalization was 43 percent. US investors held 72 percent of their portfolio in domestic stocks.[32]

According to the 2013 International Monetary Fund data, the United States only makes up about 23 percent of the world's gross domestic product (GDP). The high allocations to US markets do not make fundamental sense from an economic or market capitalization standpoint. So why do investors continue to put a majority of their eggs in the US basket? According to behavioral finance, this would be classically attributed to the *aversion to ambiguity bias*.[33] Foreign markets are less familiar to investors, and investors are wired to dislike the unfamiliar. Historically, foreign markets have tended to have higher volatility than US markets, subjecting investors to wild price swings. Since investors have both an aversion to ambiguity and losses, they tend to stay bound to their home market.

In this day and age, you need to diversify globally. Many foreign economies are beginning to invest in the infrastructure necessary to build self-sustaining economic engines that will fuel the global economy going forward. The emerging middle

32 Christopher Philips, Francis Kinniry, and Scott Donaldson, *The Role of Home Bias in Global Asset Allocation Decisions* (Valley Forge, PA: Vanguard, 2012).

33 Hersh Shefrin, *Beyond Greed and Fear: Understanding Behavioral Finance and the Psychology of Investing* (Oxford: Oxford University Press, Inc., 2002).

class offers a wealth of potential to the enterprising investor who is willing to step into the world of the unknown. As developed nations like the United States, United Kingdom, Japan, and much of Europe continue to struggle under the weight of large debt loads, many of the emerging economies are experiencing attractive growth rates.

Keep in mind that you need a disciplined approach to investing in the global markets. Meb Faber of Cambria Investment Management has done a fair amount of research on applying the CAPE ratio to global markets and has found that the CAPE is a great tool for identifying shifts in market sentiment. Meb found that investing in undervalued countries would achieve much better results than investing in overvalued countries. His study included a thorough examination of thirty-two countries since 1980. He looked at each country annually and evaluated the CAPE levels and future returns. The results are strikingly similar to the results in the United States: low CAPE values led to high returns, and high CAPE values led to low returns.[34]

A way to enhance the Value Allocator is to use the global CAPE values to determine your equity allocation among countries. Faber discovered that sorting countries based on the CAPE and investing in the most undervalued countries each

---

34 Mebane Faber, *Global Value: Building Trading Models with the 10-Year CAPE* (El Segundo, CA: Cambria Investments, August 2012).

year generated amazingly attractive returns. The results were even better when he applied a filter to the ranking and did not invest in any countries where the CAPE was above 15. For instance, if you had ranked countries according to the CAPE and invested in the top 10 percent (lowest CAPE values) each year if they were below 15, then you would have achieved returns of 18.7 percent per year after inflation from 1980 to 2011. More impressive is the fact that the maximum drop during that period was 23.4 percent versus over 50 percent for the S&P 500.

Sorting countries by CAPE is a viable method to enhance the Value Allocator approach. The US stock market is now one of the most overvalued markets in the world. It has been the most adored in the world over the past five years, almost decoupling from global markets. Many of the international markets are now the markets that offer the best long-term returns. We think the best prospects today are in the disliked international and emerging markets.

To illustrate, we have compiled expected returns, current CAPE values, and volatility measures for several countries using data from Research Affiliates in Figure 8. The inverse correlation between expected return and current CAPE value is noticeable. As expected, the higher-expected-return countries are characterized by the higher volatility and lower CAPE values. The global-value strategy is extremely difficult to apply. It takes immense fortitude to act contrary to the herd.

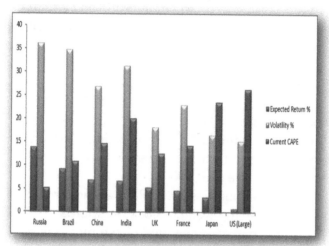

Figure 8: Expected Returns, Volatility,
and CAPE values around the Globe
Source: Research Affiliates

The Value Allocator method is designed to take advantage of undervalued markets and allocate according to a contrarian discipline. The issue is that undervalued markets can often continue to decline. We favor buying markets that are both cheap and in positive trends. You are better able to manage the risks of volatile markets by using the approach outlined in this book. The process is demonstrably flexible enough to protect your assets and at the same time intelligent enough to grow them with the market.

Adding Other Asset Classes

The trend following model we outlined during our discussion about tactical asset allocation is an oversimplified version. To recap, all we did was rank the S&P 500, Russell 2000, and US ten-year Treasury bond and then allocate resources to the strongest asset class. At the end of each month, we ranked stocks versus bonds and picked the strongest as the position for the portfolio for the next month. The purpose of the tactical portion of the portfolio is to provide diversification, hopefully yielding a more behaviorally congruent portfolio construction. The stocks-versus-bonds model demonstrated remarkable historical results, helping protect the overall portfolio during the down market years without sacrificing growth. Enhancements can be made to the tactical portion of the portfolio to generate even better results.

A number-one seller on the *New York Times* list is *Mastering the Money Game* by famed personal coach and motivational speaker Tony Robbins. It provides the reader with an outline of how to achieve financial freedom. The most interesting part of the book is the recommended portfolio allocation for investors. The portfolio is called the "all-seasons" portfolio and is supposed to be built to withstand all market conditions. The portfolio spreads the allocation among commodities, gold, US stocks, foreign stocks, and US bonds. The portfolio is similar to the risk-parity strategies made famous by hedge-fund manager Ray Dalio of Bridgewater. In risk parity, the purpose is to allocate assets equally based on risk. The goal is to combine asset classes with different fundamental characteristics, allocated based on historic volatility. The result, in theory, is a portfolio that is built to withstand bull and bear markets alike.

In order to test the concept, we constructed the all-seasons portfolio as follows: 40 percent long US-government bonds, 15 percent intermediate US-government bonds, 8 percent diversified commodities, 7.5 percent gold, 18 percent US large-cap stocks, 3 percent US small-cap stocks, 7.5 percent international stocks, and 3 percent emerging-market stocks. You can see the largest portion of the portfolio is allocated to US bonds (55 percent), as would be expected in a risk-parity portfolio.

Our efforts to test the all-seasons portfolio are not to discourage its use or discredit it. The all-seasons portfolio is a drastic improvement on the way money is typically managed in most wealth-management firms today. It removes the idea that stocks, a volatile asset class, must make up the core of your portfolio in order to get market-like returns. Essentially it is a more intelligent form of money management.

Our problem with the all-seasons portfolio is not the construction mechanism but the static nature of the program. Why would anyone want a static (buy-and-hold) approach to investing in an ever-changing world? You would not want to be holding commodities in your portfolio right now as many are off 50 percent from their recent highs. You will not want to have 55 percent of your portfolio in government bonds in the United States when interest rates begin to move up. The bond market has been on a tear for the last thirty years, and interest rates are currently at 2 percent for US ten-year Treasuries. When interest rates begin to move up, and eventually they will, investors in the all-seasons portfolio could get hurt.

We suggest taking into account valuations and trends to arrive at the optimal portfolio construction. Starting with the all-seasons portfolio, we decided to enhance our tactical portion by including US large-cap stocks, US small-cap stocks, international-developed stocks, emerging-market stocks, broad commodities, gold, real estate, corporate bonds, short-term US-government bonds, intermediate US-government bonds, and long-term US-government bonds.

We will use the same simple ranking rules that we used in the stocks-versus-bonds model and pick the top five asset classes each month. Once we rank the top five asset classes, we will equally weight each asset class, rerunning the ranking system monthly. We will call this portfolio the all asset strategy. To add a further layer of protection, we will use a risk filter, whereby we will only buy the asset class if it is above the five-month moving average of price (MA). If the asset class is below its MA, the portion earmarked for that asset class (20 percent) would be invested in US intermediate-government bonds. If all asset classes were on sell signals (below the MA), US intermediate-term Treasury bonds could be 100 percent of the portfolio. The decision tree would be as shown in Figure 9.

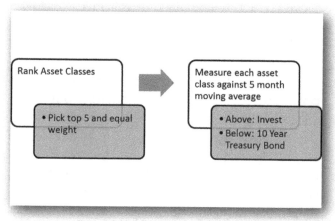

Figure 9: Adding other asset classes
to the tactical system

The ranking procedure allows the investor to capitalize on the strongest asset classes. The MA is a trend filter, investing in the asset classes when they demonstrate positive trend character-istics and avoiding them otherwise. We chose US intermediate Treasuries as the defensive asset class due to the flight-to-safety phenomenon often observed during market crashes. We were not overly concerned with inflation because we included commodities, gold, and real estate in the investable universe. Therefore, our assumption is that during inflationary periods, where bonds would have subpar performance, other asset classes would be stronger. In Figure 10, we examine the all-seasons portfolio, the S&P 500, and our all-asset strategy.[35]

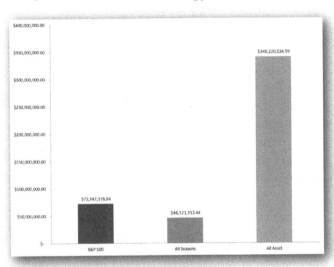

Figure 10: All-Asset Strategy (Growth of $1,000,000) 1972-2014

---

35 To calculate the returns for the all-asset strategy, we used global financial data for the index data on all asset classes up until 2007. From 2007 through 2014, we used ETF data to better replicate an investable index.

The graph has some interesting takeaways we want to point out. First of all, if you had invested $1 million in any of the three portfolios, you would have done exceptionally well over the 1972–2014 period. More importantly, investing in the S&P 500 would have been tough to stomach due to the crazy volatility. Imagine starting with $1 million in 1972 and watching that amount get cut in half in the next two years. Most likely, you would have bailed on that strategy quickly. If you had been brave enough to hold on, you would have experienced more bouts of extreme volatility in 1987, 1998, 2000 and 2008. Imagine you were about to retire in 2000, and suddenly your nest egg takes a 50 percent hit. Painful, right? Now imagine that you weather that decline and see your value reach new highs in 2007, only to experience another 50 percent decline in 2008. Looking at your account in 2009, you would realize that in ten years of investing you are down 50 percent in real terms. Most likely, your retirement plans would have to be adjusted.

The all-seasons and all-asset strategies do a great job at providing a relatively smooth ride for the investor over the forty-year period. Investors in either strategy would have been better off from a peace-of-mind standpoint. The obvious winner is the all-asset strategy, growing a $1 million investment into over $340 million. The strategy only lost money in four years, with the worst loss being 5 percent (see Table 4). The all-seasons strategy, on the other hand, would have grown to $46 million, and the S&P 500, $72 million.[36]

	S&P 500	All Seasons	All Asset
1972	18.8%	17.3%	32.3%
1973	-14.3%	0.9%	16.9%
1974	-25.9%	-1.4%	8.0%
1975	37.0%	10.0%	15.3%
1976	23.8%	14.5%	23.7%
1977	-7.0%	4.5%	11.5%
1978	6.5%	8.7%	11.7%
1979	18.5%	15.2%	35.7%
1980	31.7%	9.4%	11.2%
1981	-4.7%	-4.2%	-3.0%
1982	20.4%	29.6%	31.6%
1983	22.3%	7.0%	12.9%
1984	6.2%	9.3%	13.6%
1985	31.2%	31.2%	25.2%
1986	18.5%	25.9%	30.6%
1987	5.8%	4.3%	10.9%
1988	16.5%	11.9%	15.6%
1989	31.5%	23.0%	23.9%
1990	-3.1%	3.3%	-3.1%
1991	30.2%	18.4%	23.3%
1992	7.5%	5.8%	7.9%
1993	10.0%	17.1%	25.4%
1994	1.3%	-4.6%	-0.5%

36 All data is hypothetical and calculated with the benefit of hindsight. The data does not reflect actual performance.

1995	37.2%	27.1%	22.6%
1996	22.7%	6.0%	14.9%
1997	33.1%	12.1%	11.8%
1998	28.3%	12.4%	11.0%
1999	20.9%	3.7%	17.1%
2000	-9.0%	10.2%	8.0%
2001	-11.9%	-2.5%	-5.2%
2002	-22.0%	6.1%	5.6%
2003	28.4%	14.1%	32.0%
2004	10.7%	11.6%	11.4%
2005	4.8%	11.4%	7.1%
2006	15.6%	6.8%	22.8%
2007	5.5%	13.9%	11.9%
2008	-36.6%	2.7%	4.2%
2009	25.9%	-4.4%	30.8%
2010	14.8%	12.8%	20.2%
2011	2.1%	16.6%	17.9%
2012	15.9%	6.2%	0.9%
2013	32.2%	-4.2%	13.7%
2014	13.5%	13.7%	4.8%

Table 4: All Asset Strategy

The all-asset portfolio works well to protect and grow the portfolio versus the other strategies. The static all-seasons approach does not achieve the results of the all-asset because of the lack of dynamic allocation. The all-seasons portfolio does a wonderful job dampening volatility and achieves a similar growth rate to the overall market. The problem is that volatility is not risk, and by targeting a lower volatility, you miss out on optimal growth.

The trend following nature of the all-asset portfolio allowed the strategy to react to market changes and position itself in areas of strength. The result was that the strategy was able to protect during periods of market declines and grow the portfolio when the markets were favorable. The strategy does not require you to be an expert in the fundamentals of commodities, gold, real estate, international stocks, emerging markets, or bonds. Instead, you ride the wave when the markets are favorable, giving each asset class an equal chance to impact the portfolio.

The all-seasons portfolio illustrated that diversification works to make the ride smoother than buying the stock market. By adding momentum and trend following, you can add a dynamic component to the all-seasons portfolio to potentially better grow your portfolio.

If you believe in a more dynamic approach to investing, the all-asset strategy is a great enhancement to the tactical component of our approach. The incorporation of other asset classes such as gold, commodities, real estate, and international and emerging markets allows the overall portfolio the occasion to better weather whatever market cycle you are in. You can prosper in the up markets, the down markets, inflation, deflation, and stagflation. Combining the all-asset portfolio with the Value Allocator will potentially provide you with an optimal experience, regardless of market conditions.

Intelligent investors are superior to the typical investor in that they are in constant pursuit of a delicate balance between static and dynamic, fast and slow, and trending and contrarian. We have presented two independent but symbiotic systems that allow the astute investor to capitalize on market psychology. In isolation, the strategies are nothing spectacular, as they are extremely difficult to follow with discipline.

In fact, both the Value Allocator and trend following strategies generate a significant number of type II errors in practice. A type II error is one in which the investor fails to take the right action. On the other hand, a type I error is when the right action is taken, but the outcome proves the signal false. A false positive is another way of looking at type I errors. Type II errors are easy to make when investors are behaviorally predisposed to make wrong decisions. It takes discipline to take the appropriate action when it is mentally challenging.

Imagine for a second that you are following the Value Allocator, and it recommends allocating 70 percent to the stock market during a period such as the Great Depression. Newspapers and financial pundits are shaking your core belief in capitalism and the free market. You find yourself questioning the market and whether a recovery will ever become reality. Then you look to your program, which recommends going all in because the market is undervalued. You might hesitate, knowing that it could take years before you ever realize the gains characteristic with buying the market when it is undervalued. The failure to take this action would result in a type II error.

The tactical strategy is no different in terms of difficulty. In isolation, trend following can generate a significant number of type II errors. For instance, when a market has run up considerably, one of the hardest actions to take is to buy that asset. We are taught to buy low and sell high, not buy high and sell low. The counterintuitive nature of trend investing creates an incredibly vicious mental exercise. Trend following is a discipline to be practiced and perfected over a lifetime.

Combining the two strategies in the appropriate weightings creates a delicate dance between two opposed market forces. Value and trend following operate together to provide a portfolio that is perfectly positioned for the vibrant psychology of the market. Further enhancement through diversifying globally and adding other asset classes creates a tactic unlike any other. This system is an actively passive investment program that allows investors to position themselves to capture whatever the market has to offer, stacking the odds in their favor.

CHAPTER 6

How to Apply Our Process

It Is about "Being" the Market, Not "Beating" the Market

The data gathered over the years have demonstrated that it is extremely difficult to beat the broad market averages year in and year out. Over the last ten years, over 80 percent of active managers have underperformed their respective benchmarks. The egotistical quest to beat, conquer, and defeat the market has been a futile effort that has left a considerable fortune on the table in fees, taxes, and returns.

Investing is not about picking the right stocks or capturing temporary anomalies. As Bill and Will Bonner discussed in their book, *Family Fortunes*, investing is about *beta*. Beta, as we refer to it here, is getting what the market gets. "In the long run, it's beta that makes fortunes, not alpha. Every study proves it."[37] The evidence stacks up against trying to beat the market, as most investors, including professionals, who try to beat the market underperform the market averages over the long run.

In order to achieve success, you must remove your ego. You must lose the need to beat the market. "Most people think the secret to making money by investing is to find the stock that will go up. They all want to be an alpha investor, the big man on campus who put his money into Google when it opened for business or the guy who bought Starbucks when it went public in 1992. That's the whole game, they believe in seeking alpha."[38]

On any given day, turn on financial media on TV, and you will see the alpha craze in full effect. A talking head will no doubt discuss why he thinks a certain stock is a buy or a sell. Viewers gobble up the information as if it is going to help them make the best decisions. We are here to tell you that you are not going to derive an edge from watching financial television or reading financial newsletters. Our opinion is that you should seek an approach that makes the market your friend, not your enemy.

Index funds are investment vehicles that house a basket of securities that replicate the broad market or a particular segment of the market. The low

---

37 Bill Bonner and Will Bonner, *Family Fortunes: How to Build Family Wealth and Hold on to It for 100 Years* (New York: John Wiley & Sons, 2012).

38 Bonner and Bonner, *Family Fortunes.*

cost of indexing and popularity of exchange traded funds (ETF) have caused many investors to consider index investments. ETFs are funds that track a particular index but they trade on an exchange like a stock. The popularity of ETFs has surged over the past few years and now there are funds that track stocks, bonds, commodities, and foreign currencies.

There are several advantages to investing in ETF index funds over traditional mutual funds. ETFs are usually much less expensive than owning actively managed mutual funds. An index fund tracking the S&P 500 could be bought today for a management fee of 0.05 percent. The average actively managed equity mutual fund would cost you more than 1 percent.

The purpose of owning any investment fund is to gain the diversification that comes from owning several securities. ETF investors are able to diversify by owning a basket of securities that track a particular index. This removes the need to rely on an active manager who most likely will not be able to outperform the market.

Mutual funds trade at the end of the day because that is when the net asset value (NAV) of the underlying fund is calculated. Unlike a mutual fund, ETFs are traded over an exchange allowing them to be bought and sold like a stock. This provides the intra-day liquidity that many investors desire. In addition, there are no minimum deposit requirements for investing in an ETF meaning that investors can buy as little as one share. ETFs are making index investing accessible to everyone.

Taxes are also treated differently in an ETF versus a mutual fund. If you owned a mutual fund and shares were sold within the fund for a gain, you would have to pay taxes on that gain. In an ETF, gains on shares sold within the fund are not passed to the shareholder. The low cost, stock-like liquidity, and favorable tax treatment of exchange traded funds make them an ideal way to invest alongside the market.

If your current portfolio is invested in mutual funds, you are already playing a game where you are the patsy. In the most recent S&P Dow Jones indices versus active management report ending in 2014, 87.23 percent of domestic equity funds underperformed the S&P Composite 1500 in the past year. The last ten years yielded similar results, with 76.54 percent of domestic equity funds failing to beat the benchmark. In a study by Robert Arnott, Andrew Berkin, and Jia Ye, the researchers found that over a fifteen-year period, the average outperformance for the funds that outpaced the benchmark was only 1.10 percent. The average underperformance for the funds that failed to match the benchmark was -3.76 percent.[39]

---

39 Robert Arnott, Andrew Berkin, and Jia Ye, *How Well Have Taxable Investors Been Served in the 1980s and 1990s?* (First Quadrant, L.P., 2000).

It is hard to understand why investors continue to use active stock pickers despite the overwhelming amount of data that contradict this method. Most wealth-management firms and their advisors are largely to blame. Investors typically entrust their money to a financial advisor who hires an active manager (or several) to actually manage the money. Investors are charged higher fees that exacerbate underperformance of their portfolio. On average, they pay 1 percent to the advisor and another 1 percent to the outside managers. That is a total fee of 2 percent for an 80 percent chance to underperform the market by 3 percent, before taxes. In our opinion, skip the game and buy index funds that have average fees around 0.20 percent.

Fund Category	Comparison Index	One Year %	Ten Year %
All Domestic Equity Funds	S&P Composite 1500	87.23%	76.54%
All Large-Cap Funds	S&P 500	86.44%	82.07%
All Mid-Cap Funds	S&P Mid-Cap 400	66.23%	89.71%
All Small-Cap Funds	S&P Small-Cap 600	72.92%	87.75%
All Multi-Cap Funds	S&P Composite 1500	83.74%	84.03%

Table 5: Percentage of Managers
Outperformed by Benchmarks
Data courtesy of: S&P Dow Jones Indices LLC, CRSP 2014

Applying Our Process with ETFs

Our investment process is simple by design. The true test of any investment program comes down to execution. You may have developed the best system on paper but without proper implementation, it will not work as desired. Index funds and ETFs are ideal for applying our investment method.

The Value Allocator was tested using the S&P 500 and the US ten year Treasury bond index data. Our recommendation for imitating this portion of the strategy would be to use ETFs that track both of these indexes. The most inexpensive S&P 500 index fund is the Vanguard S&P 500 Index ETF (VOO). It has internal expenses of only 0.05 percent. The Blackrock iShares 7-10 year Treasury ETF (IEF) is a good way to follow the US ten year Treasury bond for a management fee of 0.15 percent.

You could also use the Vanguard Total Stock Market ETF (VTI) for the equity portion of the portfolio. This particular ETF is a basket of four thousand securities covering almost 100 percent of the US stock market. Furthermore, VTI covers large, mid, and small capitalization stocks and costs the same as VOO.

The Vanguard Total Bond Market ETF (BND) would diversify you across a wider array of bonds instead of solely focusing on intermediate Treasuries. BND invests in investment grade corporate, government, mortgage backed, and asset backed securities in the US. Moreover, BND costs less than IEF, maintaining a management fee of only 0.07 percent.

When using the Value Allocator in taxable accounts, you might want to consider using a tax free municipal bond index for the fixed income portion. The Blackrock iShares National AMT-Free Municipal Bond ETF (MUB) has a management fee of 0.25 percent and is designed to shadow the investment grade portion of the municipal bond market. MUB pays interest to shareholders that is federally tax free.[40] In taxable accounts this could lead to some savings as the interest paid on traditional fixed income would be taxed like earned income. Consider your tax planning and overall asset location strategy before picking the appropriate ETF.

In Table 6 we illustrate some possible allocations using the ETFs we referenced. If the market was overvalued according to the CAPE, you would allocate 30 percent to either VTI or VOO and the remaining 70 percent to BND, IEF or MUB. Your internal costs would end up being no higher than 0.19 percent. The only other costs to consider would be trading commissions which are dependent on the brokerage you use. Several brokerage firms allow certain ETFs to be traded for free.

---

40 Before implementing any tax strategy you should seek guidance from your tax professional.

	Overvalued	Undervalued
Equities	30% in VTI or VOO	70% in VTI or VOO
Bonds/Fixed Income	70% in BND, IEF, or MUB	30% in BND, IEF, or MUB

Table 6: Value Allocator and ETFs

The tactical portion of our methodology was tested using the US small capitalization index, US ten year Treasury index, and the S&P 500 index from 1972-2003. Beginning in 2003 we used ETF data to better reflect an investable index. The ETFs we used as proxies were the Blackrock iShares Russell 2000 Index ETF (IWM), the State Street SPDR S&P 500 Index ETF (SPY), and the Blackrock iShares US 7-10 Year Treasury ETF (IEF). The funds we used as proxies are not the lowest cost available. The maximum internal expense for the ETFs we used was 0.20 percent. A shrewd investor can apply the tactical system for a maximum management fee of 0.09 percent. Table 7 outlines the costs of each of these funds and possible replacements that you could use.

ETF	Market	Costs	Possible Substitutes
SPY	Large Cap Stocks	0.09%	VOO (0.05%)
IWM	Small Cap Stocks	0.20%	VB (0.09%)
IEF	US Treasuries	0.15%	BND (0.07%)

Table 7: ETFs for the Tactical Portfolio

If the tactical portfolio favored the S&P 500, you could invest in the VOO or the SPY. If small capitalization US stocks were the stronger asset class, you could use VB or IWM. Lastly, if stocks were weak compared to bonds, you could use IEF or BND to gain exposure to a defensive asset class.

The enhancements to our strategies were designed to be applied using ETFs. Adding global equities to the Value Allocator is easy to do because there are several country specific ETFs in existence. Blackrock iShares maintain the most exhaustive list of global ETFs. In Table 8 we list several of the iShares country ETFs that you could use to invest in global equities markets. If you were to apply the method we outlined in Chapter 5, you could rank each of these country ETFs by their CAPE value and pick the top 10 percent of countries (lowest CAPE) as long as the measure is below 15.

Ticker	Fund
MCHI	iShares MSCI China ETF
ECH	iShares MSCI Chile Capped ETF
EDEN	iShares MSCI Denmark Capped ETF
ECNS	iShares MSCI China Small-Cap ETF
EFNL	iShares MSCI Finland Capped ETF
EWGS	iShares MSCI Germany Small-Cap ETF
EWG	iShares MSCI Germany ETF
EWQ	iShares MSCI France ETF
INDA	iShares MSCI India ETF

EWH	iShares MSCI Hong Kong ETF
EIS	iShares MSCI Israel Capped ETF
EIRL	iShares MSCI Ireland Capped ETF
EIDO	iShares MSCI Indonesia ETF
SMIN	iShares MSCI India Small-Cap ETF
SCJ	iShares MSCI Japan Small-Cap ETF
EWJ	iShares MSCI Japan ETF
EWI	iShares MSCI Italy Capped ETF
EWN	iShares MSCI Netherlands ETF
EWW	iShares MSCI Mexico Capped ETF
EWM	iShares MSCI Malaysia ETF
EPHE	iShares MSCI Philippines ETF
ENOR	iShares MSCI Norway Capped ETF
ENZL	iShares MSCI New Zealand Capped ETF
EWS	iShares MSCI Singapore ETF
ERUS	iShares MSCI Russia Capped ETF
EPOL	iShares MSCI Poland Capped ETF
EWP	iShares MSCI Spain Capped ETF
EWY	iShares MSCI South Korea Capped ETF
EZA	iShares MSCI South Africa ETF
EWT	iShares MSCI Taiwan ETF
EWL	iShares MSCI Switzerland Capped ETF
EWD	iShares MSCI Sweden ETF
EWUS	iShares MSCI United Kingdom Small-Cap ETF
EWU	iShares MSCI United Kingdom ETF
TUR	iShares MSCI Turkey ETF
THD	iShares MSCI Thailand Capped ETF

QAT	iShares MSCI Qatar Capped ETF
UAE	iShares MSCI UAE Capped ETF
ICOL	iShares MSCI Colombia Capped ETF
INDY	iShares India 50 ETF
KSA	iShares MSCI Saudi Arabia Capped ETF
FXI	iShares China Large-Cap ETF
EWA	iShares MSCI Australia ETF
EPU	iShares MSCI All Peru Capped ETF
EWK	iShares MSCI Belgium Capped ETF
EWO	iShares MSCI Austria Capped ETF
EWC	iShares MSCI Canada ETF
EWZS	iShares MSCI Brazil Small-Cap ETF
EWZ	iShares MSCI Brazil Capped ETF

Table 8: Country Specific ETFs

Incorporating other asset classes into the tactical portion of the strategy is also easy to accomplish. In Table 9, we outline the various asset classes in the all asset strategy and give examples of ETFs you could use. To apply the strategy, you would rank all the ETFs, pick the top five, and invest in the ones that are above their five month moving average.

Market	ETF	Description
US Large-cap Stocks	VV	Vanguard Large-Cap
US Small-cap Stocks	VB	Vanguard Small-Cap

International-developed stocks	VEA	Vanguard FTSE Developed Markets
Emerging-market stocks	VWO	Vanguard FTSE Emerging Markets
Commodities	DBC	Powershares DB Commodity
Gold	GLD	SPDR Gold
Real Estate	VNQ	Vanguard REIT
Corporate Bonds	VCIT	Vanguard Intermediate-term Corporate Bond
Short-Term US Government Bonds	VGSH	Vanguard Short-term Government Bond
Intermediate US Government Bonds	VGIT	Vanguard Intermediate-term Government Bond
Long-Term US Government Bonds	VGLT	Vanguard Long-term Government Bond

Table 9: All Asset Strategy and ETFs

The explosion of ETFs has made it relatively simple to imitate our investment strategy. However, there are several tax considerations to analyze before starting. For instance, we endorse the practice of asset location within our process. Ideally an investor would want to package the tactical asset allocation system into retirement accounts where the assets are allowed to grow tax free. Thus, the investor is not penalized with short term gains when the assets are bought and sold frequently. Taxable accounts should be reserved for the Value Allocator (when possible), and investors may consider using municipal bond ETFs for the fixed income portion to lower the tax burden. There are other strategies that may help reduce the potential tax liability of implementing our approach. We recommend that you seek the advice of a qualified tax professional and plan accordingly.

Indexing is about "being" the market and controlling what you can. We think that actively managing the asset allocation process is far more important than picking the right stocks. The intelligent investor controls costs through the use of passive indexes and controls behavior and market risk through portfolio construction.

The application of the policies set forth in this book are not meant to be cumbersome. In fact, the overall approach we discuss is meant to be accomplished using ETFs.   In this chapter we not only discussed the merits of using ETFs, but provided examples of several ETFs that could be used within the confines of our system rules. Now that we have demonstrated how to execute our investment process efficiently, we are going to discuss some common investment approaches that do not work.

CHAPTER 7

Traditional Diversification
Does Not Work

Modern Portfolio Theory

Your portfolio will not be protected against large declines if all you do is diversify your holdings and rebalance. As investors found out during 2008, owning small, large, growth, value, international, and domestic stocks does not safeguard against large losses. Despite what most think, different classes of equity can and will move down at the same time. Portfolios managed in accordance with modern portfolio theory are not equipped to protect against severe bear markets.

The majority of money management firms hope to control portfolio risk by diversifying in accordance with modern portfolio theory (MPT). Harry Markowitz, in his 1952 paper, "Seminal Theory of Portfolio Allocation under Uncertainty" outlined how portfolios should be constructed.

The paper was a sensation and eventually led to Markowitz being awarded the Nobel Prize in economics. The contributions of the paper to the financial community were magnificent. In fact, Markowitz was able to articulate formulaically the effects of correlation, variance, and diversification on the portfolio returns.

The major influence of MPT involved the mitigation of risk—security-specific risk—by combining multiple assets together. The process is known as diversification, and Markowitz was able to measure the effects of diversification on portfolio risk and return. Diversification is a compelling theory from a risk-reduction standpoint. MPT established two different components of risk—systematic and unsystematic. Systematic risk is market risk, or the sensitivity of a security to the business cycle. Unsystematic risk is the risk associated with an individual investment, otherwise known as security-specific risk.

"Markowitz discovered that the unsystematic portion of risk could be eliminated by proper diversification."[41] Risky assets (stocks) are combined with less risky assets (bonds) to arrive at the optimal portfolio for an individual. Markowitz assumed that investors seek to maximize their own utility function. In other words, investors

---

41 Michael E. S. Gayed, *Intermarket Analysis and Investing*, Second Edition (Lexington, KY: Felix Culpa Publishing, LLC, 1990).

sought to generate the biggest bang for their buck when investing their money. Now, the biggest bang doesn't necessarily mean the biggest gain for your buck but instead fashions the idea that one could generate the highest return for a given level of risk.

Markowitz crafted the notion that investors seek to earn the highest level of return with the smallest level of volatility—that is, risk. When faced with two different portfolios with the same return, investors would obviously choose the portfolio with the lower variance. Given two portfolios with the same variance, investors would choose the portfolio with the highest expected return.

MPT has paved the way for a multitude of academics in finance. For instance, William Sharpe elaborated on the ideas of MPT to develop the capital asset pricing model, or CAPM. Today, it is rare that a firm does not use MPT, CAPM, or both to guide asset mix decisions. Any mutual fund fact sheet will reveal terms like *alpha*, *beta*, *correlation*, and *standard deviation*. These terms are all products of the work of both Markowitz and William Sharpe.

David Hume, Harry Markowitz's favorite philosopher and writer, said, "Truth springs from argument amongst friends." Thus, we would like to shed light on the critical shortcomings of MPT. Our effort is to lay the foundation for a better way of managing portfolios. The issues begin with how MPT defines and calculates risk. MPT assumes that risk is the variability of returns relative to a historical average. MPT assumes investors are risk averse, meaning they do not want too much variability. Variability—according to MPT—is defined mathematically by the standard deviation computation. In our opinion, standard deviation is a poor way of measuring portfolio risk. Investors do not complain to their money managers for achieving above-average returns. Most likely, investors encourage the above-average returns. Instead, investors worry more about the downside. Investors are therefore not risk averse but loss averse.

If the calculation of risk is not applicable to managing portfolios, then the diversification definitions are flawed as well. MPT uses correlation and covariance calculations to demonstrate the efficacy of diversification. By combining multiple asset classes that move differently from one another, which is called low correlation, the standard deviation of the portfolio is reduced. We have already shown the flaws associated with the standard deviation measure of risk.

Despite the obvious issues, many firms still construct portfolios by combining multiple low-correlated asset classes to achieve the highest expected return for a given variance target. Not only is the risk measure flawed, but the measurement of correlations is invalid as well. The movements among asset classes are often measured over lengthy periods of time to determine an average correlation figure. The average is then used to model the optimal portfolio.

The problem is that correlations change. We live in a dynamic world where relationships among asset classes shift in response to an almost infinite number of variables. For instance, in 2008 most asset classes moved together during the tumultuous summer months. All classes of equities (domestic and international), bonds (with the exception of Treasuries), and most commodities fell together. Portfolios managed according to MPT would have seen their risk increase dramatically during this time period. The reason is that the correlations among the asset classes increased, causing a rise in the standard deviation of the overall portfolio. For instance, a portfolio made up of 60 percent global stocks (40 percent S&P 500 and 20 percent MSCI EAFE) and 40 percent US bonds would have declined 32.83 percent from the high in 2007 to the low in 2009. A decline over 30 percent is not the type of risk a moderate investor would expect. Most investors would not have been able to handle this type of decline by staying with their investment plan. In fact, most would have probably sold during the panic, reducing their allocation to stocks at the wrong time.

Many of the failures within the banking sector during the financial crises can be directly tied to the flawed use of the mathematics common in MPT. The banks assumed certain levels of risk according to standard deviation, correlations, and the assumed normality of the data. Financial institutions failed to account for the fat tails, or the more-frequent-than-expected extreme events that often occur in the financial markets. As a result of the oversight, tons of money was lost, and the financial system was pushed to the brink of disaster.

Long-Term Capital Management (LTCM), a famous hedge fund during the late 1990s, is another sample of a massive failure to respect the nonnormal nature of the capital markets. John Meriweather, former head of bond trading at Salomon Brothers, and Nobel Prize–winners Myron Scholes and Robert Merton founded LTCM. With a star-studded lineup, they were sure to raise capital. Raise it they did, finding great success in the first few years. Their plan was to discover mispricing in various securities markets and use huge leverage to exploit for profit.

In theory, the scheme made sense. In a perfect world, mispricing corrects itself over time. The problem is that we do not live in a perfect world. In 1998, in the wake of the Asian currency crisis and Russian debt default, LTCM collapsed. LTCM's genius strategy quickly collapsed as they lost close to $5 billion in less than four months. The Federal Reserve Bank of New York orchestrated a bailout of close to $4 billion to avert what many believe would have been the beginning of a financial crisis. The fund was eventually dissolved in 2000.

LTCM failed to account for the governing mechanisms of the capital markets. The misplaced trust in normality and mathematical modeling that assumed such absurdity would eventually lead to their demise. The carnage following 2007–2009 demonstrated that such ignorance is still commonplace among financial institutions. We are afraid that further disappointment awaits those who trust their investment dollars to MPT's risky approach.

Richard Bookstaber wisely stated, "A general rule of thumb is that every financial market experiences one or more daily price moves of four standard deviations or more each year. And in any year, there is usually at least one market that has a daily move that is greater than ten standard deviations."[42] Evidence suggests that markets are not normal. The lack of normality in markets greatly reduces the effectiveness of mean-variance optimization and modern portfolio theory. An intelligent portfolio would have mechanisms

42 David Swensen, *Pioneering Portfolio Management: An Unconventional Approach to Institutional Investment* (New York: Free Press, 2009).

in place to account for extreme price movement. MPT is limited by the fact that it defines return distributions completely in terms of expected returns and variances. It fails to account for other variables such as liquidity and marketability to determine the optimal portfolio. As David Swensen discussed in his book *Pioneering Portfolio Management*, "The rigidity of mean-variance optimization fails to accommodate real world concerns." Managing money according to MPT could lead to poor results for investors.

MPT and the CAPM model support the continued progression of the art and science of investing. MPT has laid an impressive foundation for understanding the interconnectedness of different asset classes, quantifying risk and return, and revealing the importance of diversification. The shortcomings of the theory and lack of practicality only make room for improvements and innovations that will create an intelligent way to invest. We will now examine how our tactical portfolio can be an improvement over the diversification techniques of MPT.

Hedge Funds Do Not Provide Safety

Asset allocation has evolved over the years, largely on the back of modern portfolio theory. Large Wall Street firms have taken the idea of diversification to another level with the introduction of alternative investments and hedge funds. As firms understood the role of correlation in portfolio management, a new vehicle emerged—the hedge fund—designed to be combined with traditional asset classes for enhancing the portfolio. The idea is sound under the umbrella of financial theory. Pragmatism has challenged this assumption, however, and hedge-fund proliferation may have peaked during the last few years. Our assessment is that they are not necessary and that one can diversify in a simpler fashion by using trend following and momentum.

Sophisticated portfolio management has often been characterized by the incorporation of alternative strategies. The allocation to these strategies allows investors to potentially diversify a portfolio and lower overall portfolio volatility. To remain in harmony with the purpose of this book, we focus primarily on ways to get the diversification offered by these exotic investments through the use of a simpler policy. Instead of allocating across the many alternative asset classes, we rely heavily on trend following strategies to provide the appropriate diversification.

There is a large amount of support for the incorporation of alternative asset classes into the asset mix as a diversification tool. The most common asset classes referenced are private equity, hedge funds, managed futures, real estate, and commodities. The major endowments, such as

Harvard and Yale, popularized alternative investing by keeping extremely large portions of their endowments in alternatives (more than 70 percent) while achieving enormous returns. Lately, alternatives have come under fire as hedge funds have been questioned due to their underperformance of the stock market.

We are baffled by the continued speculation in hedge funds despite the costs, illiquidity, and the inability to outperform the market over the recent years. Low expected returns from both US fixed income and US equities will make it quite difficult to justify the 2 percent management fees and 20 percent performance incentives so common in the industry. Since 1990, the Hedge Fund Research Institute fund of funds composite has failed to outperform the S&P 500 and protect investors. A simpler and more cost-efficient solution exists.

The largest hedge-fund investors have taken notice of the present disconnects within the marketplace. In an article in the *Wall Street Journal*, Dan Fitzpatrick writes of a massive reduction in hedge-fund investments by the major pension plans in the United States. The reasons given were enormous fees and lackluster returns.[43]

We expect the trend to continue. The question is where the assets should be reallocated. According to a board member of one pension

---

43 Dan Fitzpatrick, "Pension Funds Eye Reducing Hedge-Fund Investments," *Wall Street Journal* (October 19, 2014).

plan mentioned in the article, Warren Buffett recommended allocating the assets to index funds. We support the notion of reducing the costs associated with traditional hedge-fund investing, but we question whether buying and holding an index fund is a better policy given the current valuations. Buying and holding an index fund would be ideal when valuations in equities were in the bottom quartile of their historical range, but they are currently in the top decile (overvalued) for the S&P 500. Under the overvalued circumstances, our recommendation is to use index funds, but through our simple strategy.

The strongest reason investors buy hedge funds is to protect themselves from market declines. Hedge funds appear attractive, as the very name indicates that they hedge the downside risk (or some of it anyway). Modern portfolio theory disciples, who govern many of the larger wealth-management firms, continue to frame hedge funds in this light, claiming that they are not correlated with equities and bonds and provide risk-reducing benefits to portfolio composition.

Unfortunately for hedge-fund investors, the data does not support the low correlation rhetoric. The correlation between the fund of fund composite and the S&P 500 from 1990 through 2014 was 0.57, indicating a moderately strong positive correlation. Even worse is the fact that from 2007 to 2009, the correlation between hedge-fund composite and the S&P

500 increased dramatically. In 2008, the HFRI fund of fund composite declined right along with the S&P 500, finishing the year down more than 20 percent. In other words, when hedge funds are supposed to "hedge," they actually acted to increase the risk of the overall portfolio.

You can achieve proper diversification without paying outlandish fees or suffering the risks associated with alternative investing. Financial theory is flawed, in our opinion, and has provided an amalgamation of complex financial products that only confuse and befuddle. Our hope is that our process will allow you to simplify your portfolio and enhance the results.

When you compare our tactical approach (see Chapter 3) to the HFRI fund of funds index, the obvious conclusion is that trend following is far superior. Tactical asset allocation is ideal for diversifying a traditional portfolio due to its ability to mitigate downside risks. Minimizing the correlations to the stock market during the down years yields a better portfolio construction. The essence of diversification is risk reduction.

The effects on the bottom line are indicated in Figure 11.[44] A hypothetical $1 million investment in the Hedge Fund Research Institute fund of funds composite index from 1990 through 2014 would have resulted in an ending value of $5,789,516.68.

---

44 All data is hypothetical and calculated with the benefit of hindsight. The data does not reflect actual performance.

The tactical portfolio, largely through the risk-reduction effects, would have resulted in an ending value of $25,915,525.21. The flexibility and protection against prolonged declines, theoretically reward the trend following strategy with superior results (see Table 10).

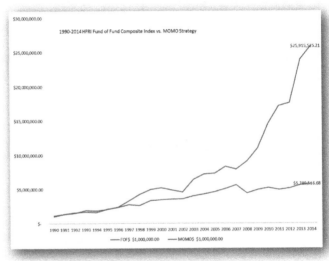

Figure 11: Trend following vs. Hedge Funds
(Growth of $1,000,000) 1990-2014

	Hedge Funds	Trend System
1990	17.5%	2.4%
1991	14.5%	36.1%
1992	12.3%	13.7%
1993	26.3%	6.6%
1994	-2.6%	-4.7%

1995	11.1%	30.0%
1996	14.4%	15.0%
1997	16.2%	37.2%
1998	-4.2%	29.1%
1999	26.5%	16.3%
2000	4.1%	5.1%
2001	2.8%	-6.4%
2002	1.0%	-5.8%
2003	11.6%	39.8%
2004	6.9%	12.2%
2005	7.5%	1.3%
2006	10.4%	13.5%
2007	10.3%	-4.7%
2008	-21.4%	14.8%
2009	11.5%	21.1%
2010	5.7%	33.2%
2011	-5.7%	17.4%
2012	4.8%	2.5%
2013	9.0%	35.9%
2014	3.4%	8.3%

Table 10: Trend Following vs. Hedge Funds

The diversification techniques of modern portfolio theory will not protect you during market turmoil. Our investment approach, by dynamically controlling the asset mix, provides a better path to diversification and overall investment success. A thorough analysis of the work of Eugene Fama will help explain some of reasons why our strategy works.

Markets Are Not Totally Efficient

In 1965, Eugene Fama, Nobel Prize winner and noted economist, coined the terms *efficient markets* and *market efficiency* in his dissertation, "The Behavior of Stock Market Prices." The paper was a model for market equilibrium and became known as the efficient market hypothesis (EMH). The premise of his theory is that prices reflect all available information.[45] In other words, price changes occur only on new information, and they do so immediately and rationally.

The idea is that current prices are a good estimate of intrinsic value and that no strategy can be used to outperform the market. Competitiveness among market participants creates market efficiency, allowing the market to reach equilibrium. The idea is that profit potential attracts new entrants quickly enough to keep prices from deviating from intrinsic value, within the bounds of rational variation.

EMH has taken the financial world by storm. The wide-scale use of index funds is largely attributed to the theory and is one of the most important contributions to portfolio management. However, according to EMH an investor is better off buying and holding an index fund replicating

---

45 Jeff Sommer, "Eugene Fama, King of Predictable Markets," *New York Times* (October 27, 2013), http://www.nytimes.com/2013/10/27/business/eugene-fama-king-of-predictable-markets.html.

the market and diversifying according to the same rules as MPT. In our view, EMH is insufficient as an investment approach. EMH has added far more to portfolio management and investing through the understanding of the limitations of the theory.

Fama and his University of Chicago colleague Kenneth French spent a great portion of their careers looking at the anomalies to market efficiency. In return, we have the Fama-French factor model. Fama and French studied market returns and determined that several factors correlated with future returns. The original three factors referenced in the Fama-French model were categorized as follows: the return spread between stocks and cash, the return spread between small capitalization companies and large capitalization companies, and the difference between cheap stocks and expensive stocks as measured by book value–to-price ratios. The idea was to use the factors to enhance the capital asset pricing model (CAPM) for determining expected returns.

Applied Quantitative Research (AQR), a prominent investment firm, has done a thorough study of the various factors in the Fama-French factor model since 1965. Several additional factors have been shown to explain returns and have been added to the model over time: the spread among the most profitable and least profitable companies, the spread among firms that invest conservatively versus aggressively, and buying strong performers and going-short weak performers.[46] The most recent findings indicate that, in terms of statistical significance, value and momentum are the strongest factors.[47] This evidence is central to our use of both value and trend following in our approach to the markets. It also shows that value and trend trading are negatively correlated, meaning that the application of both strategies in a portfolio context results in balance and sufficient diversification.

Rational Investors- The Ultimate Flaw

Financial theories are constrained by the many assumptions they contain. The most radical of all the assumptions is the belief that market participants are rational. The rational-investor assumption in MPT assumes that investors make decisions by maximizing the expected return for a given level of volatility or minimizing the level of volatility for a desired expected return.

In EMH, participants are assumed to rationally process and react to all new information so as to adequately reflect the new intrinsic value in the

---

46 Going short is the process where an investor borrows shares of a stock to sell at the current market price in hopes that they can purchase the shares at a lower price. The investor is making a bet on the stock dropping in price.

47 Cliff Asness, *Our Model Goes to Six and Saves Value from Redundancy along the Way* (Greenwich, CT: AQR, 2014).

market. EMH allows irrationality but assumes that the rational-market participants nullify the noise players—the irrational participants—to keep the market at equilibrium.

Cognitive psychologists have identified several behavioral biases that alter the way human beings process information and make decisions within an investment context. Robert Shiller, in his book *Irrational Exuberance*, illustrated the belief that the market operates on feedback mechanisms.[48] Feedback loops indicate that a positive event leads to a positive response that leads to a positive event. The same is true for negative feedback loops. The presence of the feedback mechanisms can result in deviations from fundamental or intrinsic value that last for long periods of time. When price no longer reflects an accurate measure of underlying intrinsic value, the rational-investor assumption becomes questionable. The technology and credit bubbles demonstrate anything but rationality; the market traded at extremes in both instances.

Modern portfolio theory and the efficient market hypothesis are the old ways of thinking. It is time for a new model that adapts to the ever-changing realities of the capital markets. What is needed is a method that responds and even anticipates the feedback mechanisms that so often

---

48 Robert Shiller, *Irrational Exuberance* (Princeton, NJ: Princeton University Press, 2000).

govern the investment world. Behavioral finance has ushered in a new way of thinking about investments—a method that incorporates our innate tendencies to act irrationally about money.

Our process takes into account the common biases of human cognition, creating a more efficient application of portfolio theory. Managing money according to flawed financial theory will not work in the psychological game of investing. Our methodology accounts for the common behavioral flaws that traditional portfolio theory greatly ignores.

CHAPTER 8

The Crash to Come

Valuations

What is an asset bubble? How do you spot one when you are in it? How do you protect yourself against the eventual popping of that bubble? Bubbles are periods of euphoria that cause prices to deviate well beyond what would be considered normal. Valuations are the best way to identify a bubble. Reliable measures of intrinsic value help you discover whether current prices are normal or not.

According to valuations, we are currently in the third asset bubble since 2000. Stock prices now exceed their long-term average value by a wide margin (see Figure 12). Most reliable valuation metrics suggest that if you bought the US stock market today and held it for the next ten years, you would earn only 2 percent per year on average. This is well below the 6 percent per year earned by the market since 1900. Stock prices have been driven to extreme by elated sentiment.

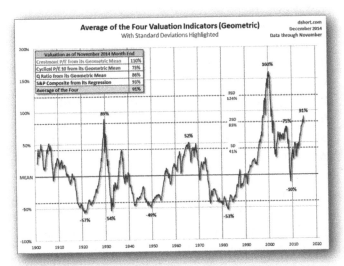

Figure 12: Average of Four Valuation Indicators
Source: Doug Short

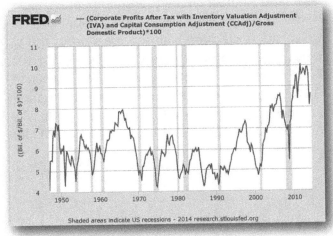

Figure 13: Corporate Profit Margins

We have spent a majority of this book examining the accuracy of the CAPE when valuing the stock market. To reiterate, the current CAPE is in the top decile of historical readings. When adjusted for the fact that corporate profit margins (Figure 13) are also in a bubble, the CAPE reading would be even more anomalous. The CAPE is not the only historically accurate valuation metric signaling caution. In the next several paragraphs we will analyze other measures that are in agreement with the CAPE.

Tobin's Q is a measure of market value that is calculated by dividing the total market value of all securities by the total replacement cost of all the companies in the market. This measure is extremely reliable, and its reliability was outlined in Russell Napier's book, *The Anatomy of the Bear*, and Andrew Smithers and Stephen Wright's book, *Valuing Wall Street*. James Tobin of Yale University is credited with the creation of the Q ratio. The Q ratio can be calculated using the Federal Reserve Z.1 Statistical Release in section B.102. It is the ratio of line thirty-nine (corporate equities) divided by line thirty-six (net worth). We have included a chart of the Q ratio since 1900 for your review (see Figure 14).

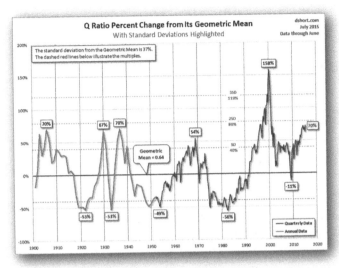

Figure 14: Tobin's Q Ratio
Source: Doug Short

You would expect intrinsic value to be one, where companies trade at their replacement cost. In actuality, the average has been around 0.7 since 1900. You will notice that sentiment extremes are accompanied by levels above 1. The highest reading was recorded during the tech bubble in 2000 when the ratio reached 1.64! As of the beginning of 2015, the ratio is 70 percent above the long-term average.

Warren Buffett's favorite valuation indicator is the market capitalization–to-GDP ratio. Market capitalization is a measure of the total value of the stock market—the number of shares outstanding multiplied by the price of those shares. GDP is a measure of the production of an economy. The formula for GDP is this: consumption plus capital investment plus net exports plus government spending. This ratio makes intuitive sense, as one would expect the growth rate of the stock market to be proportional to the growth rate of the economy. When the relationship gets out of whack, there is a deviation from fundamental value.

The market typically trades at around 70 percent of GDP. Above 70 percent, the market is considered overvalued; less than 70 percent, and it is undervalued. Sentiment extremes are realized at levels of close to 120 percent above and near 30 percent below. The highest reading is about 153.6 percent, reached in 2000. Currently, the market is trading at around 132.3 percent of GDP (see Figure 15).

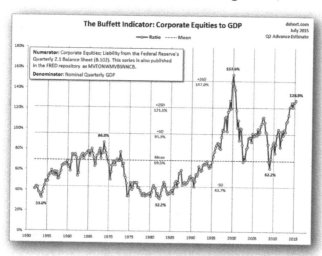

Figure 15: The Buffett Indicator
Source: Doug Short

Sentiment is obviously extremely optimistic as valuations indicate that today is the one of the most overvalued times in history for the US stock market. To add more credence to the argument, margin account levels (margin is when people borrow money to invest in stocks) are now more extreme than those of 2000 or 2007 (see Figure 16).

Figure 16: NYSE Margin Debt
Source: Doug Short

Reminiscent of most major market peaks, the psychology of the market is drastically euphoric. Stretched valuations are enough reason to take a cautious outlook on US stocks going forward. High valuations do not always mean imminent danger. In fact they are long-term indicators, and it can often take years for a market to revert to fair value. You are now equipped with a process to identify extreme moments, like today, and position your portfolio to take advantage of the probable results.

It is clear we are in a bubble. We cannot know with certainty when the bust will occur. Our process is designed to navigate the evolution of the market, whether that means further expansion or crash. Historically high valuations have led to long periods of below average returns. Thanks to easy monetary and fiscal policy, the market today is one of the most overvalued in history.

The Titanic

The economic engine that has fueled our economy since the creation of the Federal Reserve is credit expansion. Real money is leveraged up through the use of the banking system and debt to allow for increases in economic activity. The whole global financial system is dependent on credit and the continual issuance and reissuance of debt. Under the gold standard, which was ended in 1971 during the Nixon administration, each dollar in circulation had to be backed by some set amount of gold. Each dollar was a promise by the US government to pay a set amount in gold. Upon the alteration and eventual removal of the gold standard, we backed each dollar only by a law promising to pay. This is why today's currency regime is fiat-based.[49]

The Federal Reserve (Fed) has successfully maneuvered the monetary system to the point where one dollar in 1914 is worth about fifteen cents today. Similar to the Roman Empire lowering the quantity of silver in their currency, we have removed value from the dollar through a sleight of hand. Credit expansion has made our free-market participants feel prosperous, but the prosperity is not real. Dependent on credit, we now must continue to issue debt in order to maintain our standard of living.

Debt-to-GDP ratios for the major developed economies are now at levels that are unsustainable. According to the Organisation for Economic Co-operation and Development, the average debt-to-GDP ratio of the developed economies is 111 percent. According to Rogoff and Reinhart, when public debt reaches the critical threshold of 90 percent of GDP, growth usually falters.[50] Growth should be hard to come by in the largest developed nations over the long term, if history is any guide.

---

49 A fiat-based currency is a currency backed by law and the faith in the government that enforces those laws.

50 Carmen M. Reinhart and Kenneth S. Rogoff, *Growth in a Time of Debt* (American Economic Review, 2010), 573–78.

We will mostly focus on the US market, partly satisfying our embedded "home bias," and discuss the potential ramifications of runaway debt. In Figure 17, you will see a list of most developed nations and their debt-to-GDP ratios going back to 2008. If you observe the United States, it is apparent that debt is growing (see Figure 18). As our economy slowed in the 2000s, the government had to issue more debt in order to maintain the status quo. The continued expansion of debt is strangling our economic potential.

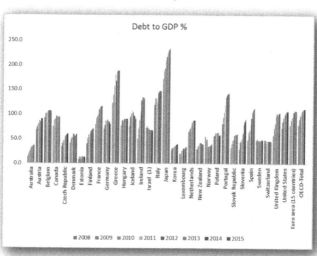

Figure 17: Debt to GDP ratios around the World

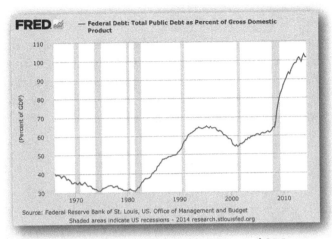

Figure 18: Total Public Debt as a Percent of GDP

Albert Einstein famously stated, "Insanity is doing the same things over and over again, expecting a different result." In other words, insanity is extreme irrationality. The US government is a perfect example of insanity. As debt grows and puts pressure on economic output, the government is forced to issue more debt to cover the rising interest expense and growing costs of managing the empire.

In 2014, 6 percent of every dollar spent went toward servicing the interest on the national debt. A whopping 69 percent went to funding major entitlements (Medicare and Social Security) and other income programs (unemployment, disability, Obamacare, and others). In fact, according to the Congressional Budget Office, entitlements and interest on the national debt will account for 85 percent of spending growth through 2024 (see Figure 19).[51] We are steering the *Titanic* directly into an iceberg, and our political leaders are content to merely rearrange the deck chairs.

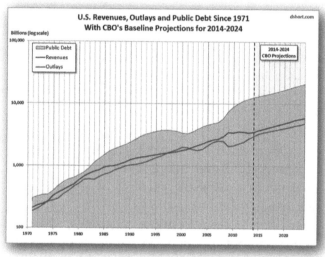

Figure 19: US Revenues, Outlays
and Public Debt since 1971
Source: Doug Short

As long as the federal outlays are above revenues, our public debt will expand. Our fear is that another recession could create a need to expand debt issuance drastically in order to offset

51 Romina Boccia, "Federal Spending by the Numbers, 2014: Government Spending Trends in Graphics, Tables and Key Points," *Heritage* (December 2014).

falling federal revenues. The situation is dire, and a difficult solution needs to be determined. The problem is that the answer will most likely be too difficult for any politician to support, because the economic law of self-interest is all too powerful.

Demographically, we are presently in a challenging environment. At the end of 2014, the youngest baby boomer will reach fifty years old. The largest percentage of our population is now reaching retirement age and will soon be taking out more money than they are paying in. As you will see in Figure 20, entitlement spending will grow exponentially and put a continuing strain on our economy, as we must issue more debt to pay promised obligations.

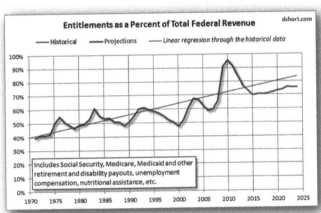

Figure 20: Entitlements
Source: Doug Short

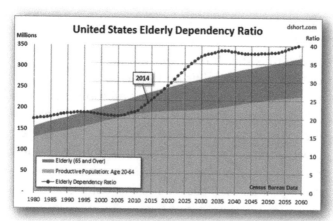

Figure 21: Elderly Dependency Ratio
Source: Doug Short

According to the Congressional Budget Office, entitlements will require 75 percent of the total federal revenue by 2025. The further we look out, the gloomier the situation appears. The elderly dependency ratio (number of elderly divided by the productive population) is set to rise considerably through 2035 (see Figure 21). We will no doubt have to continue to expand our debt to cover the increase in health care costs and entitlement spending that will result.

We think that the only way the United States has a chance of cutting debt is through inflation. Inflation would allow the United States to pay back debt with cheaper dollars, erasing part of the debt owed. The perfect political prescription would be a good deal of inflation and huge growth. The combination of both growth and inflation would reduce the debt load and increase credit availability. The problem is that inflation destroys the middle class by requiring more income to pay for the essentials of daily life. The conundrum is that inflation may help remove our debt burden, but it will strangle the discretionary spending of the US consumer. It will be difficult to generate both growth and inflation in a consumer-driven economy.

Inflation has been difficult to generate, and deflation is the predominant force. Politicians and Fed governors hate deflation because asset-price declines are difficult to stomach. On the other hand, deflation is promising for the majority of Americans because deflation creates more affordable conditions (housing, transportation, food, energy, and other items). Deflation, although having adverse effects on asset prices, would bring about a stronger dollar and better economic growth over the long term. The problem is that the pain in the short run is ghastly for politicians and threatens their ability to stay in office.

The vicious cycle is set. We are on a sinking ship where the captain and crew (politicians) do not have the ability or desire to save the passengers. We can only hope that change can be made now, but our guess is that the economic law of self-interest will continue to govern. Our addiction to debt and the illusory wealth it provides are stronger than the desire to alter our fate. If the US continues to add to the debt pile, economic growth will undoubtedly stay subpar and deflation will most likely remain the prevalent trend.

The Federal Reserve

> It is well that the people of the nation do not understand our banking and monetary system, for if they did, I believe there would be a revolution before tomorrow morning. — Henry Ford

Louis McFadden, Republican member of the House of Representatives from 1923 to 1935, had this to say about the Federal Reserve: "Mr. Chairman, we have in this country one of the most corrupt institutions the world has ever known. I refer to the Federal Reserve Board and the Federal Reserve Banks. This evil institution has impoverished and ruined the people of the United States…and has practically bankrupted our government. It has done this through the defects of the law under which it operates, through the maladministration of that law by the Federal Reserve Board, and through the corrupt practices of the moneyed vultures who control it."

The Federal Reserve is largely to blame for the great bubbles of our nation's history. Manipulating interest rates and money supply, the Fed alters the short-term course of asset prices. Since the creation of the Fed in 1914, there have been several bubbles and busts, which can be attributed largely to Fed policy. Fed policy is great at generating returns for the top 1 percent. The top 1 percent own over 50 percent of all financial assets and thus benefit from policies that produce asset-price inflation. When the Fed punishes savers through financial repression (zero percent interest rates) and forces risk taking, supply-and-demand imbalances force asset prices to increase. The problem is that asset-price inflation is a game of smoke and mirrors.

More recently, the Fed has engineered radical methods to continue to keep the credit machine churning. In economics 101, everyone is taught the law of diminishing returns. The law suggests that each additional unit of input produces diminishing output after a time. After a credit expansion that has spanned decades, output is difficult to come by. It now takes an astronomical amount of credit creation to institute the output our economy is dependent on. The Fed, knowing this, has established crafty ways to keep the credit machine operational. After the market crash of 2008, brought on by a tightening in credit that saw the global financial system almost implode, the Fed launched several stimulus programs to keep asset prices levitated. The Fed lowered interest rates to zero percent, issued loans to banks, and provided excess liquidity to the markets through quantitative easing (QE).

QE occurs when the Fed buys government bonds (Treasuries and agency mortgage-backed securities) from banks, generating liquidity for the banking system and hopefully inspiring lending. Zero percent interest rates lowered the discount rate and pushed investment forward, rewarding speculative behavior and punishing savers. The net effect was to push investors down the risk spectrum, where you had to buy higher-risk securities to generate the returns earned historically.

The first instance of QE occurred in late 2008 when the Fed launched a program to pump $700 billion into the financial system. Asset prices almost immediately responded, bottoming in March of 2009. QE 1 ended in the spring of 2010, and the market quickly reacted by dropping almost 20 percent. The flash crash of May 2010 shocked the investment community, as many of the world's best companies saw their stock prices drop ridiculously in minutes. Overall, the market nosedived over 6 percent in the month of May.

The Fed quickly responded by launching QE 2 in the summer of 2010, providing more provocation to the now-addicted market participants. Again, a much larger program would be required to provide the necessary elixir to a growth-starved market. QE 2 took the market to new heights, only to end during the European debt debacle in the summer of 2011. The credit crisis overseas, the end of QE 2, and the downgrade of US debt created a perfect storm that took the S&P 500 down over 20 percent. The bear market chatter began, and helicopter Ben Bernanke, the Federal Reserve chairman at that time, came to the rescue. He launched Operation Twist, another form of QE, and QE 3 began one year later in 2012.

QE 3 ended in October 2014. The question is whether or not the markets will follow historical patterns once stimulus is withdrawn (see Figure 22). The punch bowl is now gone, and you should be on guard. The market may not be able to stand without the additional credit creation introduced by the Federal Reserve. Interest rates are still at zero, but rate increases are now being debated and are expected during 2015. The problem is that the market may interpret the absence of additional monetary support as tightening, causing risk aversion to become commonplace. QE has done nothing other than increase the risk appetite, sacrificing forward growth for current return. The result has been massive wealth inequality; only those parties who could participate in asset-price increases were able to prosper.

Figure 22: Fed Intervention
Source: Doug Short

The Fed has injected the market with ridiculous amounts of liquidity and has become the buyer of last resort for US debt. Their actions have provided the confidence needed for investors to embrace risk taking. The situation is ultimately a game of confidence with the quest to restore faith in the US financial system.

The Fed's policies, like zero percent interest rates (see Figure 23), have done nothing to positively impact middle-class America. Zero interest rate policy (ZIRP) is actually a form of financial repression where the Fed punishes savers eventually forcing yield seeking behavior. The desired outcome is that the wealth effect, through increases in asset prices, takes hold and restores confidence in the economy.

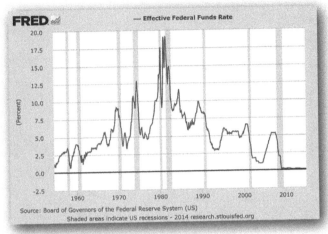

Figure 23: Zero Percent Interest Rates

Asset-price inflation only benefits the asset owners though. The net result is that the rich get richer while the majority of the population gets poorer. Aggregate hourly earnings are a great predictor of future economic activity. If hourly earnings are growing, consumption is mounting. Since we are a consumption-driven economy, if consumption is rising, our economic output (GDP) is increasing. Therefore, moderate wage inflation is great for the economy and is accompanied by increased demand. Since the Great Recession, average hourly earnings have been largely flat. Therefore, consumption has been below trend, causing growth to be disappointing (see Figure 24).

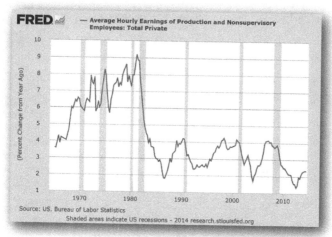

Figure 24: Average Hourly Earnings

Since 2000, hourly earnings have averaged a paltry 2.5 percent gain per year. At the same time, the number of billionaires in the world has increased from 470 in 2000 to 1,645 at the end of 2013. The middle class, the hard-working backbone of the US economy, is faltering while the elite are growing stronger because of credit expansion policies.

Evidence suggests that the wealth effect tactics of the Fed have not worked to increase inflation and halt deflation. The price of oil per barrel has declined over 50 percent in 2014. The reason oil is down 50 percent has everything to do with the US dollar (see

Figure 25). The dollar is up against most global currencies because of the end of QE and other global central banks easing policy. The fact that our Fed is debating tightening policy sometime in 2015 while others are easing policy is creating a massive global market distortion. The stronger dollar is therefore pushing oil prices down as they have a strong inverse correlation to one another. Essentially, if the dollar goes up, oil prices move down. If the dollar moves down, oil prices rise.

Oil price inflation has strangled the American middle class in the past because it requires a higher percentage of earned income to pay for energy. Lower oil prices means more disposable income, which means more consumption. Consumption is the key to economic growth in the United States. So what is the problem? The problem centers back on the fact that the global economy is heavily dependent on debt and credit. As oil prices collapse, oil companies (especially smaller enterprises) have extreme difficulty being profitable.

Smaller companies rely on access to credit markets for working capital and operational expenses. As losses pile up, defaults begin to rise. Defaults bring about credit shocks, and credit shocks generate crashes. As we speak, energy companies have fallen precipitously from their peak prices, some declining over 50 percent. Countries tied to oil exportation, such as Russia, Venezuela, and many Middle Eastern nations, have seen their markets crash as well. In a tightly interwoven global economy, it does not take long for contagion to surface and crashes to spill over into more stable assets, like US stocks.

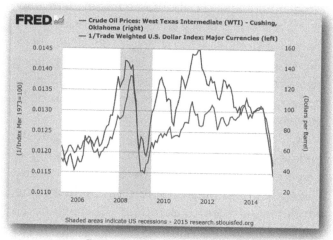

Figure 25: Oil and the US Dollar

Deflation is not only evident in the price of oil. Industrial metals, precious metals, and agricultural commodities have all seen massive price declines because of falling global demand and an increasing dollar. The Fed's efforts to create demand through liquidity injections have failed to prevent the inevitable. Commodity prices are illustrative of the powerful force of deflation as prices have plunged across the board. We expect deflation to spill over into other risk markets, such as stocks.

Prices for raw materials have been dropping over the last year in response to the rising dollar and slow global growth. Copper is often referenced as an economic bellwether because copper prices often follow global economic development. As industrial production picks up globally, copper demand surges, putting pressure on supply and causing prices to increase. Therefore, when the price of copper falls, it is often a sign that global economic activity is dropping. Copper is not telling an encouraging story at the present moment (see Figure 26). With deflation dominating the global markets, we think the risk assets will be extremely sensitive to shocks. The largest shock to the global markets could come in the form of monetary tightening by the Federal Reserve.

Figure 26: Copper Prices

Will The Fed Pop The Bubble?

What happens when the Fed stops stimulating the markets, by raising rates or selling bonds held on their balance sheet? Our guess is that the market could not handle the end of the massive stimulus. The Fed has expanded their balance sheet to over $4 trillion, only recently slowing their rate of expansion as they wound down QE 3. If the punch bowl were suddenly taken away, the market could crash in dramatic fashion. We think it will be difficult for the Fed to fully step away from the market.

Many of the most celebrated economic milestones during the most recent recovery have been identified in the employment indicators. Labor market improvement has been one of the most cited reasons to begin tightening monetary policy among Federal Reserve board members. On the surface it appears as if the labor market is improving. The unemployment rate has fallen from over 10 percent to lower than 6 percent in the last six years. The problem is that the employment-to-population ratio is as low as it was in 1975 (Figure 27). Over seven million people have dropped out of the labor force since the Great Recession, and the result has been a precipitous drop in the unemployment rate. The employment picture is not as healthy as the unemployment rate suggests.

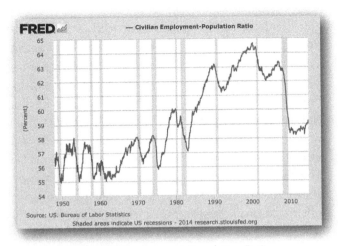

Figure 27: Employment-Population Ratio

Two members of the New York Federal Reserve, Gauti Eggertsson and Benjamin Pugsley, wrote a paper in 2006 entitled "The Mistake of 1937." In the paper, they said, "The economic conditions can be summarized as follows: 1) There are signs that the depression is finally over. 2) Interest rates have been close to zero for years but are now finally expected to rise. 3) There are some concerns from both policy-makers and the market participants over indications of excessive inflation. 4) This is of particular concern to some who point to a large expansion in the monetary base in the past several years as well as the current bank holdings of large excess reserves."[52]

---

52 Gauti Eggertsson and Benjamin Pugsley, "The Mistake of 1937: A General Equilibrium Analysis," Federal Reserve Bank of New York, 2006.

The economic conditions today are remarkably similar: (1) It has been six years since the end of the Great Recession, and the labor market has shown signs of recovery; (2) Interest rates have been zero since 2008, and now the Fed is debating raising interest rates; (3) Market participants, pundits, and policy makers are worried about the likelihood of runaway inflation; and (4) The Federal Reserve has increased their balance sheet to over $4 trillion in the past few years in efforts to provide stimulus and generous liquidity to a wounded economy.

As in 1937, the economy has been in a recovery due to the easy money and accommodative stance of the Federal Reserve. Asset prices have increased dramatically, and confidence has once again returned to the capital markets. In 1937, monetary policy and fiscal policy tightened prematurely, and the effects were frightening. From 1937 through 1938, the economy entered into a deflationary spiral where GDP collapsed by over 9 percent, industrial production slumped 40 percent, and the stock market rapidly lost half of its value.[53]

Janet Yellen should not make the same mistake as the one made by the Fed in 1937. We have shown you that the economy is sluggish, global growth is slowing, and deflation is the dominant force. Several

---

53 Eggertsson and Pugsley, "The Mistake of 1937."

global central banks have cut rates or increased asset purchases so far in 2015.

Many developed economies are even now operating at negative real interest rates. Asset prices have surged, but growth and inflation are nowhere to be seen. The solution has been to keep pushing interest rates further into negative territory and continue enlarging central-bank balance sheets. At the same time, the United States is debating whether to tighten policy. It is our opinion that the Fed should wait until inflation is obvious before beginning the process of increasing rates. To alter policy at this point would only create an acceleration of the deflationary effects that have seen oil collapse from $100 to $43. Inflation is a formidable foe, but deflation is hard to stop.

The Fed, the European Central Bank (ECB), the Bank of Japan, and the Bank of England have been extremely aggressive in expanding balance sheets to combat the rise of global deflation. The Fed has led the way with creative financing, leveraging their balance sheet to a level that would rival Long-Term Capital Management. Quantitative easing, loan programs, and zero percent interest rates set the stage for other central banks to ease conditions as well. The central banks of the developed nations have all worked to fight deflation and reflate asset prices.

The problem is that deflation has been strong, with most European nations on the brink of recession and Japan still trapped in the grip of a twenty-year deflationary trend. The ECB has announced a massive QE program of their own at the beginning of 2015 with hopes to counteract the vicious decline in economic output currently witnessed in the Eurozone. Global central banks obviously believe that the solution to the addiction of debt is to issue more debt.

In the world of investing, irrationality is plentiful. The top professionals in the industry, and amateur investors alike, share in the insanity of the markets. Human psychology governs the marketplace, and the casual observer may never recognize the ebbs and flows of sentiment as the market swings from irrationally exuberant to despairingly despondent. The long cycle of the market sees investors take the market from bubble extremes to incredible crashes over and over again. Enough time lapses between bubble and burst for short-term memories to be overwhelmed by the hype of the day.

The psychological state of the market today is that of euphoria in the United States. The stock market is now extremely overvalued, according to several different measures. In 1929, 2000, and 2007, valuations were at levels similar to today. The Fed has pushed forward returns into the low single digits for the next ten years, and now investors are faced with an almost certain debacle.

Imagine if you were set to retire in 1929, right before the market collapsed 85 percent, only to see it recover twenty years later. What about 2000, where a fall of over 50 percent has happened not once but twice since? How scary would it have been to retire in 2007, right before Bear Stearns collapsed, Lehman Brothers failed, and the global financial system reached the brink of implosion?

We are in the midst of another Fed-induced asset-price bubble, like the technology and real estate ones before. Unsustainable debt levels, stretched valuations, slowing global growth, deflationary forces, and poor demographic trends suggest a crash is ahead. We only hope that you can quickly implement an approach like the one outlined in this book to shield your wealth against potential danger. It is liberating to know that you no longer have to rely on the Federal Reserve to keep the markets up, as you can adapt to whatever occurs and prosper in the long run.

CHAPTER 9

Conclusion

Investment success can be boiled down to constructing an intelligent, dynamic portfolio that readily adapts to prevailing market conditions. In fact, the approach we have outlined in the prior pages can be applied easily. You do not need to stay glued to CNBC or read every investment newsletter.

If you want to achieve long-term triumph, the key is the avoidance of big mistakes. You now have the tools to measure when the crowd is at an extreme and take advantage of the limitations of the human brain. We have also demonstrated how to use trend following to capitalize on herd mentality and avoid painful loss aversion. A disciplined process that avoids emotional decision-making, when applied over and over again, will be successful.

Stay guarded against the expert opinion. They are more vulnerable to emotional decisions because of the illusion of knowledge and overconfidence bias. Our advice is to follow a disciplined, rules-based process that is long-term in nature and implementable. We are confident that we have provided you with such a program.

Right now, the US stock market is in the middle of another great bubble. The tech bubble, the credit bubble, and now the QE bubble all generated substantial risk taking that took markets to euphoric extravagances. Throughout market history we have seen that when markets reach periods where psychology is too sanguine, the subsequent years are often painful. The problem is that it is hard to time exactly when the eventual crash will come.

Assuming you are an investor with a moderate risk tolerance and long time horizon, the Value Allocator would recommend an allocation of 30 percent to stocks and 70 percent bonds as of the end of 2014. The tactical portfolio, as of August 2015, would recommend an allocation to the 10 year Treasury bond. Essentially, the environment would be described as overvalued and in a negative trend. Therefore, as of August 2015, our strategy would be invested 15 percent in stocks and 85 percent in bonds. The market has been overvalued since the end of 2012. If the trend were to change, which can happen quite rapidly, it could recommend 65 percent stocks and 35 percent bonds. These portfolio weightings assume that half of the portfolio is positioned in the Value Allocator and the other half is managed tactically. The right proportion in each system is dependent upon your objectives, constraints, and personality. We recommend seeking out the guidance of a fiduciary advisor if you need assistance.[54]

The process that we outlined includes two key decisions. The first decision would be made annually based on the valuation of the overall market. In the system we discussed, we would examine the market versus the historical rolling-median value and allocate more than our benchmark if undervalued and less if overvalued. In this book, we assumed a moderate investor with a benchmark of 50 percent stocks and 50 percent bonds. If the market were overvalued, we would invest 30 percent in stocks and 70 percent in bonds. If undervalued, we would invest 70 percent in stocks and 30 percent in bonds. Applying the global enhancement would mean that we carve out something like 40 percent of our equity to be applied to global markets. The portfolio matrix would be as follows:

	Overvalued	Undervalued
US Stocks	18%	42%
Foreign Stocks	12%	28%
US Bonds	70%	30%

The global stocks would be chosen based on the ploy outlined by Meb Faber where an investor

---

54 Go to www.cfainstitute.org/learning/investor/adviser/ Pages/index.aspx for more information.

would rank countries by the CAPE and invest in the top 10 percent of countries (lowest value) if their CAPE was below 15.[55]

The second decision would be made on a monthly basis. This strategy would be to rank each asset class by price return and pick the top performer. This would provide the tactical portion of the portfolio that would diversify the core, allowing you to keep more of what the market gives you while protecting against market crashes.

The all-asset enhancement could be applied by picking the top five asset classes according to the ranking system and equally investing in those asset classes. Furthermore, you would ensure that each asset class was in a positive trend by applying a moving-average filter. The purpose of the all-asset portfolio is to allow for better diversification by adding more asset classes like commodities, foreign equity markets, and gold.

Jim Cramer once stated that you should spend one hour per week per stock you own. Most academic literature suggests that a diversified portfolio consists of at least eighteen stocks. That means that, at the bare minimum, you would have to spend eighteen hours per week in order to maintain the knowledge necessary.

---

55 Mebane Faber, *Global Value: How to Spot Bubbles, Avoid Market Crashes, and Earn Big Returns in the Stock Market* (The Idea Farm, LP, 2014).

That is preposterously complex in our opinion. All you need to understand is how much you should put in stocks, bonds, and diversifying strategies. You do not need to understand the supply chain, read three-hundred-page quarterly reports, listen to conference calls, travel to company headquarters, read every analyst report, talk to consumers, or know the CEOs personally. You only need to be the market and protect against the downside.

Peter Bernstein once said that "investment success not so much accrues to the brilliant as to the disciplined." Discipline is the most critical missing link when it comes to success. Our hope is that you can take these methods and apply them with fortitude, confidence, and unwavering discipline. Discipline is painful at times. It means that you follow the rules regardless of the outcome. Committing to a process and doing it with repetition is critical to achieving the desired effects.

An intelligent investor will have a mechanism for investing offensively and defensively. In our approach we have defined clear-cut buy and sell rules for guiding your asset allocation. Traditional diversification, based on flawed financial theory, will not protect you during periods of market stress. In the last 15 years, the stock market has declined more than 50 percent on two different occasions. During both of those declines, diversification failed to protect portfolio assets.

Portfolio construction and asset allocation must evolve to our ever-changing world. You can rest assured that our process is responsive to the evolving psychology of market participants. As long as investors make emotional decisions, you will be able to spot extremes in behavior and avoid the big mistakes.

The Value Allocator serves as our core investment guide. Using value to determine the proper asset mix protects portfolios from dangerous investor behavior, positioning the portfolio in a stance contrary to the masses. Furthermore, it protects against market turmoil, as crashes are often associated with extreme valuations.

We incorporate trend following to complement the Value Allocator and provide a mechanism for tactically allocating assets. The long-term nature of value investing makes it challenging to stick with. Trend following is used to further protect portfolios in the down markets while allowing the flexibility to capitalize on intermediate-term opportunities. Adding a tactical component mostly alleviates the behavioral hurdles to a successful investment plan.

This book has examined our approach during periods of inflation, deflation, stagflation, rising or falling interest rates, and strong or weak economic activity. Now it is up to you to implement the program and, most importantly, follow it with discipline. Visit www.wealthshieldadvisor.com for more information on how you can implement our process.

BIBLIOGRAPHY

"Growth in a Time of Debt"*American Economic Review* 2010 573-78

Behavioural Investing: A practitioner's guide to applying behavioural finance West Sussex, EnglandJohn Wiley & Sons Ltd.2007

Benchmarks as Limits to Arbitrage: Understanding the Low-Volatility Anomaly*Financial Analysts Journal* 2011 40-54

Beyond Greed and Fear: Understanding Behavioral Finance and the Psychology of Investing Oxford Oxford University Press, Inc. 2002

*China: Slower Growth, but a Bigger Economy*www.huffingtonpost.com/steven-barnett/china-economy-growth_b_5105990.html

*Devil Take the Hindmost: A History of Financial Speculation*New York Penguin 1999

Dshort-Advisor Perspectives www.advisorper-spectives.com/dshort

*Eugene Fama, King of Predictable Markets*http://www.nytimes.com/2013/10/27/business/eugene-fama-king-of-predictable-markets.html

Extraordinary Popular Delusions and the Madness of Crowds New York John Wiley & Sons 1996

Family Fortunes: How to Build Family Wealth and Hold on to It for 100 Years New YorkJohn Wiley & Sons 2012

Federal Spending by the Numbers, 2014: Government Spending Trends in Graphics, Tables, and Key Points Heritage www.heritage.org/research/reports/2014/12/federal-spending-by-the-numbers-2014

Freakonomics: A Rogue Economist Explores The Hidden Side of Everything New York, NY William Morrow2005

Global Value: Building Trading Models With The 10-Year CAPE El Segundo CA Cambria Investments

Global Value: How to Spot Bubbles, Avoid Market Crashes, and Earn Big Returns in the Stock Market The Idea Farm, LP 2014

Good to Great: Why Some Companies Make the Leap and Others Don't New York HarperCollins 2001

How Well Have Taxable Investors Been Served In the 1980's and 1990's? First Quadrant, L.P 2000

Intermarket Analysis and Investing Lexington, KY Felix Culpa Publishing, LLC 1990

Investment Psychology Explained J Wiley & Sons 1993

Irrational Exuberance Princeton, NJ Princeton University Press 2000

Long-Term Investors and Valuation-Based Asset Allocation *Applied Financial Economics* 2012

Market timing in regression and reality *Journal of Financial Research* 2006 293-304

Money Master The Game 7 Simple Steps to Financial Freedom New York Simon and Schuster 2014

Our Model Goes to Six and Saves Value From Redundancy Along the Way" Greenwich AQR 2014

Pioneering Portfolio Management: An Unconventional Approach to Institutional Investment New York, NY Free Press 2009

Point and Figure Charting: The Essential Application for Forecasting and Tracking Market Prices Third Edition Hoboken, New Jersey John Wiley & Sons 2007

S&P Dow Jones Indices LLC, CRSP S&P Dow Jones indices versus active management report Report 2014

Technical Analysis: The Complete Resource for Financial Market Technicians FT Press 2010

The Case for Momentum Investing Greenwich AQR 2009

The Hedge Funds: Wall Street's New Way to Make Money *The Institutional Investor* 1968

The Intelligent Investor New York HarperCollins 1973

The Ivy Portolio: How to Invest Like the Top Endowments and Avoid Bear Markets New York John Wiley & Sons2009

The Little Book of Trading: Trend Following Strategy for Big Winnings Hoboken, New Jersey John Wiley & Sons, Inc.2011

The Mistake of 1937 New York New York Federal Reserve 2006

The role of home bias in global asset allocation decisions Valley Forge, PA Vanguard2012

The Winners of the New World www.thestreet.com/story/891820/1/the-winners-of-the-new-world.html

Thinking, Fast and Slow New York Farrar, Straus and Giroux 2011

Trend Commandments: Trading for Exceptional Returns Upper Saddle River Pearson Education, INC. 2011

Trend Following: Learn to Make Millions in Up or Down Markets Upper Saddle River Pearson Education Ltd 2009

Value Investing: Tools and Techniques for Intelligent Investment West Sussex, UK John Wiley & Sons 2009

Valuing Wall Street: Protecting Wealth in Turbulent Markets New York McGraw-Hill 2000

Wall Street Journal Pension Funds Eye Reducing Hedge Fund Investments

Winning The Loser's Game: Timeless Strategies for Successful Investing New York McGraw Hill 2010

Yes, You Can Time the Market Hoboken John Wiley and Sons 2003